Living in God's Light

Living in God's Light

Susan E. Willhauck

ABINGDON PRESS / Nashville

LIVING IN GOD'S LIGHT
by Susan E. Willhauck

This book is printed on acid-free, elemental chlorine-free paper.

ISBN: 0-687-02197-9

MANUFACTURED IN THE UNITED STATES OF AMERICA

03 04 05 06 07 08 09 10 11 12—10 9 8 7 6 5 4 3 2 1

Contents

About the Author

Susan E. Willhauck is assistant professor of Christian formation and directs the lay education program at Wesley Theological Seminary. She is an ordained deacon in The United Methodist Church. Prior to teaching at Wesley, she served a number of congregations in the ministry of Christian education.

Susan loves teaching and writing, especially poetry. She is married, has two teenage children, and lives in Fairfax, Virginia.

A Word of Welcome

Welcome to Living in God's Light. This five-session study will introduce you to several biblical stories that present God's presence using the image or the metaphor of light. Moses experiences the call of God in the burning bush (Exodus 3:1–4:17). God leads the people through the wilderness in a cloud by day and a pillar of fire by night (Nehemiah 9:9-15). God's light comes in the birth of Jesus (Luke 1:28-38; 2:1-33). Jesus reveals God's light in conversation with Nicodemus and in his reference to himself as "the light of the world" (John 3:1-21; 8:12; 12:35-36). Paul experiences God's light in a life-transforming experience on the road to Damascus (Acts 9:1-20). God's light attracts, guides, arrives, reveals, and shines in our lives. We respond to, trust in, rejoice in, believe in, and reflect God's light. In every instance the Scriptures reveal a key aspect of relationship with God and what it means to *live* in the light of God.

A FEW TIPS ON THIS RESOURCE

Living in God's Light is suitable for an intergenerational teaching setting, such as Vacation Bible School, which may meet for two hours or more, or for a 45-to-60-minute study session on Sunday morning or during the week. Writer Susan E. Willhauck is a devoted fan of Vacation Bible School and sees this experience as "a unique time for adults to learn together and a time for adults and children to learn from one another. It can offer the opportunity to do some different things: to try some new teaching and learning styles, to learn in an intergenerational setting, to take more time to ponder the Scripture and to reflect theologically."

Whether you decide to use the book as a stand-alone Bible study resource or for an adult study at Vacation Bible School, Willhauck suggests that you purchase a blank book to use as a personal journal during the study.

UNDERSTANDING THE DESIGN

The main text includes the commentary on the biblical text with further thoughts on its meaning and application for us. In the left margin you will find a purpose statement, a reminder of how the teaching options are identified, and activity suggestions that meet the needs of a variety of learning styles among participants. Each session includes suggestions for intergenerational activities.

Activities identified with ❁ indicate teaching suggestions that form the core learning for a session. Every section in the main text has at least one core option, which is on the left side of the page, with the same (or abbreviated) subhead as the section to which it refers. Choose from among these core activities. Activities in **bold italics** need extra time or preparation to do and may require added resources, such as a Bible atlas, dictionary, or commentary. These can be used if you have time and can obtain the needed study tools or art supplies.

ENJOY!

LIVING IN GOD'S LIGHT offers many opportunities for you to discover the beauty and value of living in relationship with God as "illuminated" in the Scriptures. Our prayer is that you delight in the wonder of God's light in Scripture, in the world, and in your life.

Chapter 1

$\mathcal{T}$he Burning Bush

Exodus 3:1-8, 13-15; 4:10-16

GATHERING MOMENTS

❀ Greet participants. Pray responsively the selections from Psalm 27.

Light a candle to remind you of the presence of Christ. Sing the hymn "Turn Your Eyes Upon Jesus."

PURPOSE

To understand how God called Moses through the burning bush, how Moses responded, and how we respond to God's light.

THE SESSION PLAN

Choose from among the core teaching activities (identified with ❀). Add options in **bold italics** to extend beyond a 45- to 90-minute session.

GATHERING MOMENTS

The LORD is my light and my salvation;
　　whom shall I fear?
The LORD is the stronghold of my life;
　　of whom shall I be afraid?

Hear, O LORD, when I cry aloud,
　　be gracious to me and answer me!
"Come," my heart says, "seek his face!"
　　Your face, LORD, do I seek.
　　Do not hide your face from me.

Teach me your way, O LORD,
　　and lead me on a level path.

I believe that I shall see the goodness of
　　the LORD
　　in the land of the living.
　　　　　　(selections from Psalm 27)

SETTING THE SCENE

The Book of Genesis ends with Joseph's reassurance to his brothers before his death: "God will surely come to you, and bring you up out of this land to the land that he swore to Abraham, to

SETTING THE SCENE:
❋ Read Exodus 3:1-8, 13-15, and 4:10-16 aloud. Review the actions that led Moses to Midian. Review the events leading up to the story.

Show a video clip of the burning bush from *Moses* from The Bible Collection (Turner Home Entertainment) or from other movies about Moses. Check your public library, church library, or neighborhood video rental store for possibilities. Make sure you follow copyright regulations for viewing the clip. Cue up the tape to the scenes of Moses' call in the wilderness. If you watch more than one version, compare the similarities and differences in the films' interpretation of this story. What do you think the film director is emphasizing in each case?

Isaac and to Jacob" (Genesis 50:24). He asked that his bones be carried out of Egypt. Exodus opens by telling how the Hebrews had multiplied; and because they were so numerous, the pharaoh in Egypt felt threatened. So the pharaoh "oppress[ed] them with forced labor" and instructed the midwives to kill boy babies. Exodus 2 records the infancy story of Moses. Pharaoh's daughter rescued him from the river and raised him with the help of his mother and sister, Miriam. When Moses was a young man, he killed an Egyptian and fled from Egypt to Midian. There he met a priest who had seven daughters. Exodus 2:18 tells us that the priest's name was Reuel. (Exodus 3:1 gives Jethro as the name, and Judges 4:11 calls him Hobab.) Moses settled with the Midianites and married Zipporah, one of Reuel's daughters. All this adventure in two short chapters!

The Book of Exodus tells of God's actions to free a group of people from slavery and to unite them into a community. The Exodus is central to the Hebrews' understanding of themselves. Exodus has been called "the birth story of Israel as a people."[1] In the Jewish tradition the annual Passover meal recounts events of the Exodus handed down from generation to generation.

The Exodus story is so much more than a nice story to tell the children. Moses is more than a character in a movie, played memorably by Charlton

10

Heston or "beautifully animated and brought to the silver screen by Steven Spielberg," as the trailer for *Prince of Egypt* says. Jews and Christians understand the Exodus as the story of all people, especially those who have experienced any kind of oppression or bondage and have been set free by God.

God's light appeared to Moses in the burning bush. For those who read or hear the story, light provides a powerful image for God's presence. We connect with the light of God as that which frees us from darkness.

THE THEOPHANY

God's appearance to Moses is called a theophany, which is a "God-sighting." The location of the theophany is interesting. Horeb, the mountain of God, is beyond the wilderness. The word *Horeb* means "wasteland." In the Bible, God comes to people in specific locations, which include fields and wastelands. God is not vaguely "everywhere" but specifically present in a physical place. *The New Interpreter's Bible* says that elsewhere in the tradition, the "mountain of God" is referred to as Sinai and that the Hebrew word for bush (*seneh*) may be an allusion to Sinai (Volume I; Abingdon, 1994; page 711).

As Moses tended sheep on Horeb, the "mountain of God," a blazing bush caught his eye. The fire attracted his attention, and he "turned aside" to see

THE THEOPHANY
Using a Bible atlas, locate Egypt on a map in relation to Midian and Canaan. In those ancient times, the main method of transportation was walking. It was an ordeal to move animals and people through such terrain. Talk about some of the risks of such a journey. What does it mean to you to say that God comes to people in a particular place?

❀ Talk about any "burning bush" experience that you may

11

have had. Consider the following questions: What do you think it would take for God to get our attention? Do you think God still comes to us in burning bushes? How so?

Paint a picture of the burning bush. Use watercolors or tempera paint on stiff paper to express how you think the burning bush might have looked to Moses. Do not worry about being artistic. Tell about your painting. What do you think Moses thought or felt as he saw the burning bush?

Look up St. Catherine's Monastery online. The web address is *www.interoz.com/ egypt/Catherines.htm.* Print out and show pictures of Moses and the burning bush. Another depiction of the event is in the *Golden Haggadah of Passover,* a richly illustrated prayer book for Passover created in Spain in the fourteenth century.

why the bush did not burn up. God's light attracts. The angel of the Lord appeared to Moses, and the divine voice came through the bush that was burning, "but was not consumed." The word for "angel" (*malak*) often indicated God, who was sometimes unrecognized. God's extraordinary word to Moses came from a bush that would not burn up.

In the Bible, fire or light is often the form of a divine appearance. Not only did Moses see the angel of the Lord, he heard God speak. God warned Moses to "Come no closer!" and declared the place holy ground. The removal of footwear in sacred places was an ancient custom and remains so today in many cultures. (See Joshua 5:15.) Today, Buddhists and Muslims remove their shoes before entering a holy place. In some Asian homes, family and guests remove their shoes upon entering.

God identified himself to Moses, and Moses hid his face because he was afraid. In Western society we often stress the value of making eye contact for effective communication. In some cultures it is an affront to look another person directly in the eye. A Chinese woman who came to the United States was amazed at how young people look directly at their elders when speaking to them. She explained how that would be considered disrespectful in her culture. Also, in some African countries, men and women do not look each other in the eye.

(See the images on the World Wide Web at *http://www. manuscriptcollec tion.com.)*

❊ Discuss the characteristics of God in the story of the burning bush. When have you experienced God as one who evokes dread or fear? as one who cares deeply about human suffering? as formal and distant? as near to you and accessible? In each of these experiences, how have you come to know and experience God as "I AM WHO I AM"? How does our tendency to see God only as a friend distort our image of God? What other stories of the Bible tell of humans' attempts to "get too close" or to become God? When have you or someone else you have known tried to fly too close to the sun?

This vision of God in the fire evoked fear and dread. Moses recoiled at this mysterious power. We often think that the miracle in this story occurred when God appeared in the fire, but it is the second part of that sentence "yet it was not consumed" that really says more about God's power and mystery. This mystery is imperishable. God will not burn up and turn to ashes. God will not be all used up, but will endure forever.

Today, the notion of God as one who produces fear and dread is not a popular one. We prefer to think of God as our friend, as a kind and gentle soul. Yet the mystery that is God also inspires fear and deep reverence. The light of God causes us to squint because of its intensity. Our eyes are not accustomed to it, yet we are attracted to it. We fly around the light like moths. Icarus, a character in Greek mythology, was so taken with the delight of flying that he ignored his father Daedelus's warning and flew too close to the sun. He fell from the sky when the warmth of the sun melted the wax on his wings.

When God's people tried to become like God or to get too close to God, they got into trouble. Consider the narratives of Adam and Eve and of the Tower of Babel (Genesis 1-3; 11:4-9). Humans and God are distinct, and God's presence rightfully inspires awe. Being in the presence of God does not make Moses feel warm and fuzzy. It does not give him a sense of comfort or peace. Rather, it calls him to a dangerous opportunity.

PURPOSE AND IDENTITY

PURPOSE AND IDENTITY

❀ In small groups research names for God in Bible study resources such as the *Harper Collins Bible Dictionary, The Interpreter's Bible Dictionary,* or *Eerdmans Dictionary of the Bible.* Check with your pastor or your church library for the resources. Look up *Yahweh; El Shaddai; adonai; names for God; I AM WHO I AM; Tetragrammaton.* Write the biblical names for God on a large sheet of white paper. Beside them list what other names that you have for God. Compare them to the biblical names.

God stated the purpose of the encounter with Moses: "I have observed the misery of my people who are in Egypt; I have heard their cry" (Exodus 3:7). So God came down to deliver them, to bring them to a land flowing with milk and honey. God claimed to know the suffering of the people. The Hebrew word for the verb *to know* (*yada ti*) may denote the intimacy of marriage or shared experience. Here we have "the other side" of God, the one that knows humans intimately and cares about human suffering. The God of awe, mystery, and intense light is also open to our wounds and to our pain. God, who speaks to us from a bush that does not burn, is one who communicates a sense of awe and mystery and a sense of intimacy and deep compassion.

Moses' response is something like, "Who, me?" or "Why me?" He questions God, "What if I go to the Israelites and say that God has sent me and they ask which god?" The ancient world was polytheistic. With multitudes of gods available, why this one? Moses' question was legitimate. Moreover, Israel's ancestors called God by many names. God answered with a word play on the verb "to be" (*hayah*), commonly translated, "I AM WHO I AM." It can also be rendered, "I WILL CAUSE TO BE WHAT I

Create a humorous skit of the dialogue between Moses and God. Look for the humor that exists in Exodus 4:1-17. How might the dialogue go if Bill Cosby or another comedian were playing the role of Moses? Present the skit to a wider audience.

WILL CAUSE TO BE," which indicates God's creative power. The Hebrew for "I AM WHO I AM" reads *ehyeh asher ahyeh*. Some scholars believe that this is not really a name, for the name of God was never spoken. The structure of the phrase is similar to YHWH, which is called the *Tetragrammaton*, a Greek word that means "having four letters." Since the Hebrew alphabet does not contain vowels, we do not know exactly how this would be pronounced. Some scholars say "Yahweh"; others say that by tradition, the name of God was not supposed to be pronounced at all. Until the destruction of the Temple at Jerusalem, the name of God was permitted to be spoken only by the High Priest and only in the Holy of Holies inside the Temple and then only once a year on Yom Kippur, the Day of Atonement. Sometimes a Jew will call the deity *HaShem*, which simply means "The Name." Many Bibles use the term "Lord" for the YHWH. In any case, the Tetragrammaton, or God's self-identification, is a promise for presence. The name says that God is, that God will be, that God causes to be, and that God will cause to be. In other words, the God who exists and who creates is with us and will always be with us.

CALL AND OBJECTIONS
❀ Read Exodus 4:1-17. Locate and list Moses' objections in

CALL AND OBJECTIONS

This story, like other stories of God's call in the Bible, follows a pattern that goes something like this:

the text and God's response to each objection. Alongside those, list and discuss when you have made similar objections to serving God. What were God's reassurances of your objections?

Invite participants to close their eyes and imagine themselves as Moses. Tell them to try to see, hear, smell, taste, and feel the elements of the story. Read Exodus 4:1-17 aloud. Stop at opportune moments. Ask: What does the scene look like? What do you hear? smell? taste? feel? Continue with another section of text. Pause. Repeat the questions. When you have finished reading, say: "When you feel ready, open your eyes." Invite participants to tell the group what they experienced during the reading.

1. The divine presence is made known.
2. God calls someone.
3. The person raises objections.
4. God rejects or addresses those objections and offers reassurance.
5. The person accepts the call.

God called Moses to act in God's stead to save God's people. Think about it. God asked Moses to go back to Egypt, a place he ran away from after having killed someone. Moses must have thought, *Do I really want to go back there?* God told Moses, a fugitive from justice, to return to Egypt and to lead the people into the wilderness to worship God. The objections Moses raised may refer to past experiences of his own limitations, but God helped him to see a new future.

We all have those "tapes" we play: "I'm too fat," or "I always freeze in front of a crowd," or "I'm not smart enough." Moses, in desperation, argued, "I have never been eloquent. . . . I am slow of speech and slow of tongue" (Exodus 4:10). The Lord answered with some rhetorical questions, "Who gives speech to mortals? . . . Is it not I, the LORD?" (4:11).

Notice that God does not say to Moses, "I will make you eloquent." God simply says, "I will be with your mouth and teach you what you are to speak" (Exodus 4:12). Moses will not be eloquent on his own power; God will tell him what to say. The Lord promises to be *with Moses' mouth*.

Then in one last feeble attempt, Moses

16

begged, "Please send someone else." From the text we get the sense that God's patience just ran out. God is angry, but resorts to "Plan B." Aaron shall accompany Moses and serve as his mouth.

Moses did not give an acceptance speech upon receiving God's call. The text says that he went to his father-in-law to ask permission to go back to see his people. Even though Moses was adopted by the Egyptian pharaoh's daughter, he knew that he was a Hebrew. He knew who his people were (Exodus 2:11; see also Hebrews 11:23-25). Moses was entrusted with taking his people to a new land. An old African proverb from Ghana says, "If you do not know where you are going, at least know where you have come from." Moses was certainly not sure where or why he was going, but at least he knew where he came from. He decided to answer God's call. God would light the way.

OUR OWN BURNING BUSHES

❀ If you are keeping a journal for this study, write about the account of the burning bush from the perspective of Moses. Respond to the following questions: What would you identify as "burning bushes" in your life? How have you experienced God's call?

OUR OWN BURNING BUSHES

I have heard the story of the burning bush all my life. It is truly one of the most significant signs and wonders of the Bible. To tell the truth I have always found it more than a little strange and unsettling. I admit part of me has had a "yeah, right" attitude about this story. Bushes do not just burst into flames and not burn up. On the other hand, I am profoundly jealous of Moses' theophany. Another part of me wants to scream, "Moses, you've just seen

How do you experience God's call now? When do you respond to God as Moses did?

Discuss ways your group might answer God's call to help liberate people. Identify contemporary circumstances that suggest being enslaved or in bondage such as those in prison, the homeless, or those who suffer addictions. What ministry could you commit to in the days to come? Plan how you will engage in this ministry. Pray daily for any who are in bondage.

a burning bush and heard God speak! What's your problem?"

I would like my own burning bush. I have a saying that often crosses my lips, "God, don't be subtle." A neon billboard would be nice. If I saw one, would I turn aside to see as Moses did? I wonder, though, if I have looked for a burning bush in all the wrong places. When I think about it, God has come to me through many people and experiences. God's presence in my life is indubitable, though sometimes, I admit, I am just not paying attention. When I think about it, I have experienced God's call in miraculous ways, just going about my business. Elizabeth Barrett Browning expressed this in her famous lines:

> Earth's crammed with heaven,
> And every common bush afire with
>   God.
>
> (from "Aurora Leigh")

God is among us. Will we see and know?

The call of God is central in the Christian life. God calls all people. God calls some of us to step forward as leaders. God calls people to a diverse assortment of ministries, all in service to God's kingdom. Our reluctance to answer the call is often because we think we are not worthy or we are afraid that we will not do well. Mother Teresa is credited with saying, "God does not call us to be successful. God calls us to serve."

Moses would not always be successful.

18

The Hebrew people drifted away from God and complained bitterly most of the way to the Promised Land. Moses served God despite their unfaithfulness.

The fact remains that God does call us. The question is not "Is God calling me?" The question is, "What is God calling me to do?" We can ignore the call or deny it or not understand it; but like the bush, it is still there. The light of God still blazes.

TWO PERSPECTIVES IN THE TEXT

There are at least two perspectives or voices in this text that contribute to the composite testimony of the people. One emphasizes the role of God. The other emphasizes Moses' response. Both perspectives need to be considered to understand the story. The two different perspectives may not always be easy to identify, but may be outlined as follows:

TWO PERSPECTIVES IN THE TEXT

❋ Read the text again silently to yourself. See if you can identify the two perspectives in the text, and jot down the verses for each perspective.

Do more research on the text. Check your library for commentaries. Raise any new

Perspective 1	Perspective 2
Tells the story, concerned with moving along the narrative, uses imagery	Enters as a second voice
Emphasizes the actions of God for the accomplishment of divine purpose	Views God as more remote, employing angels or intermediaries; humans respond with fear and reverence
God acts through natural agents	Emphasizes commissioning Moses to bring forth Israel
Stresses the people's need for deliverance	Stresses Moses' authority as a leader of the people

insights you gain from reading the commentaries. Discuss their relevance for understanding the story.

THE PROMISED LAND
Share a meal of milk and honey and other biblical foods. Bible reference books or an Internet search may help you identify appropriate foods.

❀ Discuss the following: What visions do you have of "the Promised Land?"? How do we think of the United States as the Promised Land? How do we fall into the trap of "affluenza," the "disease" or condition of consumerism and materialism that pervades our society? What moral choices can we make to contest affluenza? How have your perceptions of the Promised Land changed?

CLOSING TIME
Construct a display ahead of time. You will add an item to the display each session. For

THE PROMISED LAND

God described the land where the Hebrews were to go as a land "flowing with milk and honey" (Exodus 3:17). The country of the Canaanites, descendants of Canaan, is described in Genesis 10. Exodus 12:25 and 32:13 refer to this land as that which God promised to the Hebrews. When we think of the Promised Land we may have visions of blissful abundance and overflowing bounty. To a nomadic people, milk meant simply good pastureland and honey was a natural product of wild bees. The promise was for a land that would provide sufficiently for their needs, not for a life of luxury. The promise was not for unearned wealth, but for that which was needed to live. The promise was not for physical ease, but for what would satisfy the human heart. The promise for the land of milk and honey did not mean that God would bless the people by making them affluent, or that certain people must be blessed because they have it all. God promised to provide all that is needed for life, and God's provision did not relieve the people of responsibility.

CLOSING TIME

The story of Moses' encounter with God in the light of the burning bush speaks to us in many ways, on many levels. One way to express its meaning is

20

the first item, bring in a shrub or other plant in a pot. Give each person 4 x 8-inch squares of red and yellow tissue paper. Have them write a word or phrase from the lesson on each square. Tell them to crinkle the tissue and place it in the bush one person at a time. Have each person say his or her word aloud before sticking the paper in the bush. Display the burning bush in a visible place in your church.

❀ Write a free verse prayer. Free verse is a form of poetry without the usual rules of form and rhyme. Start with images, and remember it does not have to rhyme. Read these aloud as your closing prayers.

through poetry, which becomes prayer. Here are two examples of some reactions to the story in free verse:

Example 1:
God, who will not let us go
We, like Moses, have run out of excuses.
We have seen your great light.
We have felt the blazing flames of your spirit close.
We now know that if you provide
We will go.

Example 2:
Burning God,
Show yourself to me
In the dark of night,
come as fire and light.
Will I be ready?
Will I hide my face?
Will I go where you send me?

---

[1]Bruce C. Birch, Walter Brueggemann, et. al, *A Theological Introduction to the Old Testament*. Nashville: Abingdon Press, 1999, page 99.

INTERGENERATIONAL ACTIVITIES

Make silhouettes of Moses and the burning bush. Place a makeshift biblical headdress on a person and have that person stand sideways in front of a sheet of newsprint taped to a wall in a darkened room. Shine a flashlight to cast a shadow. Trace around the shadow to draw a profile. Cut out the silhouette to use as a pattern. Adults will cut out additional silhouettes from black construction paper. Children will cut out "flames" from orange, red, and yellow paper. Create pictures by gluing the flames behind the profile on another sheet of paper. Adults and children talk together about the story.

Gather outside at night, and look up at a streetlight or spotlight. Talk about how the bright light cuts through the darkness. See if moths or other creatures fly close to the light. Adults talk with the children about what attracts God's creatures to the light. Ask, "What attracts us to God?" and "How is God the light of the world?"

Chapter 2

𝒜 Light to My Path

Nehemiah 9:9-27

GATHERING MOMENTS

❀ Greet participants. Pray responsively the selections from Psalm 119.

Light a candle to remind you of the light of God in Christ. Sing the hymn "Open My Eyes That I May See."

Add to your display. Place a lantern or an open Bible in the burning bush display. (See pages 20–21.)

PURPOSE
To learn that the people of God remembered how God's light led them despite their rebellion and how God's Word lights our way.

GATHERING MOMENTS

The writer of Psalm 119 extols the benefits of following the way of God. Selected verses from that psalm lead us into the text for this session:

Happy are those whose way is blameless,
    who walk in the law of the LORD.

How can young people keep their way pure?
    By guarding it according to your word.

I will meditate on your precepts,
    and fix my eyes on your ways.

Open my eyes, so that I may behold
    wondrous things out of your law.

Teach me, O LORD, the way of your statutes,
    and I will observe it to the end.

Your statutes have been my songs
    wherever I make my home.

THE SESSION PLAN
Choose from among the core teaching activities (identified with ❋). Add options in **bold italics** to extend beyond a 45-to-60-minute session.

Your hands have made and fashioned me;
  give me understanding that I may learn
    your commandments.

Your word is a lamp to my feet
  and a light to my path

Keep my steps steady according to your
    promise.
                    (Selections from Psalm 119)

The hymn "Open My Eyes That I May See," written by Clara H. Scott in 1895, is a prayer that asks God for illumination. It begins by asking God: "Open my eyes that I may see / Glimpses of truth, thou hast for me."

We pray that we may see the truth God has for us. The light of God helps us see; and it illumines us, that others might see God through us.

SETTING THE SCENE
❋ Take an initial poll on what people know about Nehemiah. Ask participants who they think Nehemiah was. Review the background for the Book of Nehemiah in "Setting the Scene."

❋ Make a list on chalkboard or large sheet of paper of the things God did for the people recalled in

SETTING THE SCENE

Some scholars connect the Book of Nehemiah with the previous Book of Ezra, believing that the two were originally one book. Others disagree and cite the theological differences between the two writers. Both Ezra and Nehemiah report events that took place in the post-exilic period that scholars place around 539 to 430 B.C. Second Chronicles ends with the conquest by the Chaldeans, the destruction of Jerusalem, and the carrying away of the Temple treasures. The

24

Nehemiah 9:9-27. Make a second list of some things that God has done or does for us today. Discuss similarities and differences between the two lists. Save the lists for the closing time.

Read Nehemiah 9:9-27 aloud. Dramatize the reading by having someone dress up and appear as Ezra before the assembly. Point out that this speech took place in a worship gathering of the entire community.

conquerors took many leading citizens of Jerusalem into exile in Babylon. When the Persians came to power around 539 B.C., their emperor, Cyrus, called for the exiles to return to Jerusalem to rebuild the city and the Temple. The return to Jerusalem took place in stages with Sheshbazzar leading the first stage. Efforts to rebuild the Temple were opposed by the traditional enemies of Judah in Palestine. After several attempts, it was finally completed during the reign of King Darius of Persia (Ezra 6:14-15).

Nehemiah was a Jewish official in the service of Emperor Artaxerxes. Nehemiah was appointed governor of Judah and charged with rebuilding the city wall around Jerusalem. Nehemiah directed and organized the rebuilding of the city wall; he also played a role in restoring honor to the city of Jerusalem and re-ordering the community of the faithful. After the story of rebuilding the wall, Nehemiah 7 includes a list of those who returned to Jerusalem.

The Temple had been rebuilt, the wall had been completed, and the people were gathered. A celebration commemorating restoration and reconstruction began with a reading of the Torah. Nehemiah 8 identifies the reader as Ezra, a scribe and a priest. After the people heard the reading of the Torah, they resolved to study the law and they made a covenant to walk in God's law. Ezra led

Look in a Bible dictionary for more information on the Babylonian Exile, King Cyrus, the Festival of Booths, Artaxerxes I and II, and Ezra.

the people in a celebration of the Festival of Booths. The Festival of Booths (*hag hassukkot*) had been a harvest or ingathering festival, and the booths represented the temporary shelters that were constructed in the fields during the time of harvest. Ultimately, it became a celebration of the Exodus.

In Chapter 9 of Nehemiah, the Israelites engaged in penitence or confession with fasting and the donning of sackcloth. The Levitical priests called the people to "Stand up and bless the LORD." The Scripture for this session occurs within Ezra's communal prayer that recounts the historical experiences of the people with considerable emphasis upon the Exodus. The return to and restoration of Jerusalem after the Exile is sometimes referred to as the "second exodus."

Ezra prayed as an act of renewal for the community. In his prayer, he pointed to the light of God that led them: "You in your great mercies did not forsake them in the wilderness; the pillar of cloud that led them in the way did not leave them by day, nor the pillar of fire by night that gave them light on the way by which they should go" (Nehemiah 9:19).

REMEMBERING

REMEMBERING
❋ Tell favorite family stories. Set a time limit for each story. You may also want to do this as an intergen-

Groups of people often understand and define themselves by the stories they tell. As the worship in Nehemiah

The Holy City

Today the people of Jerusalem and the immediate sur-
roundings suffer because of political unrest and violence
in the Middle East. The enduring conflict between the
Israelis and the Palestinians is well known. This lesson
does not go into the political aspects of that conflict; but as
we study this passage, we cannot help but feel the bitter
irony of this historical setting and story. People everywhere are saddened by the lost lives and suffering in this
city that is such a central part of the three religions of the
Book: Christianity, Judaism, and Islam. We mourn to see
holy shrines destroyed. The faithful are reluctant to make
pilgrimage to the Holy Land because of war. We cry out
for peace, but know that there are no easy answers to this
prolonged discord. Astronaut Neil Armstrong, the first
human to walk on the moon, reportedly said that walking
in the Holy City of Jerusalem, where Jesus might have
trod, was more of a thrill even than taking those first steps
on the moon. We continue to pray for peace.

erational activity. Why do you think the act of remembering is important? How can we remember without living in the past? How do you deal with painful memo-ries? How do you think painful memo-ries can offer opportu-nities to know God?

remembers what God did for the people, our worship today remembers what God did through Jesus Christ. Worship "re-members" or "puts together again" the events of the Christian story. But it is also more than remembering; our worship also calls forth our future in God's care and love. A word for the act of remem-bering, *anamnesis*, derived from a Greek form suggests the activities of identity formation and of naming one's purpose and what gives meaning to one's exis-tence in addition to the activity of recall-ing events. *Anamnesis* is soul-memory. As

Listen to the song, "Memory" from the musical, Cats. Pay attention to the lyrics. In the play, this scene is set on a lonely street corner under a street lamp. The singer reflects on the past, but also on "a new day." How does the imagery of light and darkness come out in this song? What does it say to you about the importance of remembering?

opposed to *amnesia*, or the inability to recall who one is, *anamnesis* is remembering the story of where you came from and calling that into present reality. Our memories may be happy ones, or they may be very painful. Still, our memories shape who we are. The initial joy of the worshiping people that the Book of Nehemiah describes turns into mourning at the remembrance of their sin and rebellion.

In Book 11 of the *Confessions*, Saint Augustine rejects the common linear understanding of time with three divisions of past, present, and future.[1] He asserts that past, present, and future are aspects of the same reality in trinitarian relationship. We all probably know that in the experience of boredom time stretches out and seems like an eternity; yet in the experience of excitement and passion we lose all track of time, and hours pass by like moments. The time passed may be the same on a clock, but our experience of the time may be quite different. A person's faith is connected to the past. The past is always present to us, always a part of us. The future is "not yet" but it is already forming in our lives. For the returned exiles, remembering where they came from was essential in order to empower them to obey God's commandments and to rebuild their place of worship. God's reputation had endured for generations of kings of Israel and Judah and through the period of the

Exile. Ezra said of God, "You made a name for yourself, which remains to this day" (9:10b).

LIGHT ON THE WAY

Ezra addressed God and identified God's important acts: You led them by day with a pillar of cloud, and by night with a pillar of fire, to give them "light on the way by which they should go" (9:19). The symbols of the pillars of cloud and of fire are used several times in the Hebrew Scriptures to describe how God was with the people on their journey. Both the pillar of fire and the pillar of cloud reveal a protective God who leads the people.

Have a time of silent prayer in which you try to put aside all thoughts and images and focus on the mystery of God. Do you find this way of praying difficult or easy? Why? What insights do you gain, if any, from this kind of prayer?

The pillar of fire, according to the *New Oxford Annotated Bible*, may reflect the custom of carrying a burning torch at the head of an army or caravan to show people far back in the line the direction in which to walk. (See Exodus 13:21; Numbers 10:11, 34; Deuteronomy 1:33; and 1 Kings 8:10-11.) We may think of clouds as being light and fluffy like cotton candy; but in the Exodus story, the image of a cloud is powerful. The "pillar of cloud" guides and protects.

❁ Draw a path representing your life from birth to the present on a plain sheet of paper. You may also do this in your journal. The path may take many turns and have many hills and valleys. Along the path draw

The pillar of fire communicates how God shows the way in the darkness of night. In Chapter 1, I quoted an African proverb: "If you don't know where you are going, at least know where you have come from." Another spin on that is "if you don't know where you are going, any

---

Contemplative Prayer Practice

A fourteenth-century work by an unknown British monk, *The Cloud of Unknowing*, describes Christian contemplative prayer practice.[2] The writer advocated putting aside all images of God and meditating and praying without a physical image of God in mind. The truth that this type of prayer recognizes is that God is ultimately mysterious and infinitely more than any human image can represent. In the Exodus story, God was neither the fire nor the cloud, rather, God was "in" the pillar of fire and the pillar of cloud (Exodus 13:21).

---

flames to represent particular instances or times when you have experienced the light of God. Beside each flame write a word or phrase identifying that time. Take turns telling about these experiences.

path will work." The message of the text is, however, that God showed them the path. God provided a light. God revealed the path. In the same way, our faith is a revealed path. Figuratively speaking, God's light leads us where God wants us to go.

In the early church, those who sought to become Christians were initially called *inquirers*. Often they were called *rudes*, because they were viewed as rough and uninformed. After receiving instruction, they were called the *photizomenoi*. Those who completed the period of intense instruction were the *illuminati*. Those who sought baptism were referred to as the *electi* or *competentes*. The metaphor of light is embedded in the roots of *photizomenoi* and *illuminati*.

It was not easy to become a Christian, yet more and more decided to follow the light and to live the Christian life.

LIGHT AND SHADOW

LIGHT AND SHADOW
Discuss the problem of negative under-standings of black-ness or darkness. What are some exam-ples of how we do this? What are some positive ways of con-trasting good and evil, life with or without God?

Look at some paint-ings or black and white photography. Look at still-life paint-ings, the photographs of Ansel Adams, or other art that uses light and shadow in

The Bible uses the imagery of light and darkness to contrast life with God and a life without God. All metaphors have their limits, however; and today we question the persistent tendency to assign negative value to darkness or blackness. Understanding blackness as bad or evil is, to many people, racist. Can we avoid assuming that lightness or whiteness is better and cherish all of the multiple hues and shades of color in our world? In order to fully appreciate and understand lightness, we need the con-trast of shadow. Understanding God as providing light in the darkness may not necessarily contribute to a societal mis-understanding of blackness. Artists know the value of shadow to enhance the light in a painting. Still-life paintings often rely on the contrast of light and shadow for their beauty.

Two experiences provide illustrations. On a spelunking expedition, a young Boy Scout got separated from the rest of the group. Deep in the bowels of a cave, he stopped to look at something, got behind, and then took a wrong turn. He called out and tried to catch up with his troop. He continued walking for a while, but then his flashlight batteries dimmed and completely died. He was surrounded by darkness. He had been trained by his Scout leader not to panic in a crisis situa-tion, so he simply sat down and waited. He later told about this adventure and interesting ways. Another excellent resource is *Landscapes of Light: An Illustrated Anthology of Prayers, Photographs,* by Robert Cooper (Paraclete Press, 2002). Your local public library may have art and photography books. Show the contrast between light and shadow. What role does light play in the pictures? How about shadow? How do light and shadow contribute to the beauty and power of the work of art?

❋ Talk about experiences of being in the dark, both literally and figuratively. How did you find your way in these times? Write about these experiences in your journal.

LAW AS LIGHT
❋ Discuss the variety of meanings for ordinances, laws, statutes, and commandments.

described how he had never before experienced such complete and total absence of light. In the darkness and silence of the damp cave he prayed that someone would find him. Despite his great fear, he felt peace in the darkness.

Eventually the Boy Scout was missed and rescued. When his rescuers came, he was never happier to see a glimmer of light. Walking out of the cave into the bright light of day, he found the light painful. He had to close his eyes for several minutes. The experience became a metaphor for life for this young boy. Being in the cave brought him closer to God. Even in darkness, we can find the light of God. The darkness makes the experience of light more intense.

I once attended a midnight New Year's Eve Watch Night service in Nigeria. Most of the worshipers were black, and since electricity was scarce, the church was dark. The service began in a dark silence, then moved into joyous praise with singing and dancing. Only a few dim candles actually provided light, but the church seemed awash in a bath of light. I have never seen so much fire and spark generated in the darkness. The Bible affirms that God gives us light to break in upon the darkness and show us the way of truth.

LAW AS LIGHT

The text recalls how God came down upon Mount Sinai and gave the people

What do you see as the value of God's law as presented in Nehemiah 9:13? In what ways do we resist or have a negative opinion of God's law? What insights do you gain about God's law from Nehemiah 9:13?

"right ordinances and true laws, good statutes and commandments" (Nehemiah 9:13). The Hebrew words translated "ordinances," "statutes," "laws," and "commandments" in the NRSV offer a tapestry of meanings. The word that is translated "ordinance" is *mishpat*, which carries the sense of a legal judgment or verdict. The "ordinances" ("judgments" in the KJV) are right or just. "True laws" is the translation for *'emeth towrah*, which says God's laws are more than simply "true." The "laws," especially those of the Ten Commandments and the laws included in the first five books of the Old Testament, are "faithful," "trustworthy," and "sure." *Choq* or "statute" means an appointed task or decree as well as a law and thus carries a very active and directive sense for those who obey the statute. "Commandment" is a close translation for *mitsvah*. "Good" is the English word used to describe both of these words, and it is a pale translation of *towb*, which has many more specific meanings: joyful, beautiful, cheerful, gracious, pleasant, and kind are among them.

The law of God was given to provide light on the way. The psalmist also expressed this view: "Happy are those whose way is blameless, / who walk in the law of the LORD," and "Your word is a lamp to my feet, / and a light to my path" (Psalm 119:1, 105). God gave ordinances, laws, statutes, and commandments not so much as "legislated rules"

Create a mural contrasting society's laws with the law of God. Tape a long sheet of mural paper to a wall. Draw a line down the middle of the paper and label one side "Society's Laws" and the other side "God's Law." Look through recent newspapers or news magazines for headlines or news stories about people making or breaking society's laws. Cut these out. Using glue sticks, paste them to the "Society's Laws" side. Look for headlines about people following or not following God's law. Cut these out and glue them to the side marked, "God's Law." Discuss the news stories you found as examples of both. What does this activity say to us about how we follow God's law? Display your mural in the church.

but as a gift of light and a guide for the journey. The revealing of the law was the revealing of the way of God.

Often we do not really like laws. Or, we only appreciate law when it guarantees the punishment of someone who wrongs us. We resist being confined by laws or being told what to do. Sometimes we feel that law is oppressive. We see law as legalism or extreme, literal enforcing of the law. Sometimes we see law as the opposite of grace.

Paul called for obedience to law at the same time that he expressed belief in salvation by faith in Romans 3. Romans 6:14-15 acknowledges the importance of both grace and law with respect to sin. Further, while Paul acknowledged that believers are free from law, he said that law taught the meaning of sin (7:7) and that law is holy (7:12). On the other hand, he wrote to the Galatians that all who live by works of law live under a curse because of this teaching: "Cursed is everyone who does not observe and obey all the things written in the book of the law" (Galatians 3:10). However, Paul gave validity to law as God's way of dealing with human transgression. Paul said that law guarded the people and served as disciplinarian until Christ came and faith was revealed (3:24).

Paul summarized the argument about law in a way that evokes the teachings of Jesus: "For the whole law is summed up in a single commandment, 'You shall love your neighbor as yourself' " (5:14). In Matthew's Gospel, Jesus said, "Do not think that I have come to abolish the law or the prophets; I have come not to abolish but to fulfill. For truly I tell you, until heaven and earth pass away, not one letter, not one stroke of a letter, will pass from the law until all is accomplished" (Matthew 5:17-18).

The Great Commandment captures the "heart" or essence of all of God's law: " 'You shall love the Lord your God with all your heart, and with all your soul, and with all your mind.' This is the greatest and first commandment. And a second is like it: 'You shall love your neighbor as yourself' " (22:37-39).

Law is not opposed to grace, rather, the laws of God were seen as good and were given *out of grace* to free us. What a tremendous gift! Law is a good thing. It is light for our path. Again the psalmist sings, "I will meditate on your precepts, / and fix my eyes on your ways" and "Oh, how I love your law! / It is my meditation all day long" (Psalm 119:15, 97).

LEAVING THE LAW
❋ Read Nehemiah 9:9-27. List all that the prayer says God did for the people. How did the people respond to the light of God's generosity? What are some of the ways we are "stiff necked" today? What

LEAVING THE LAW

Nehemiah 9:16 marks the stark contrast between what God has done for the people and how the people failed to obey the law. This section of the text expounds the cycle of rebellion and deliverance. They acted presumptuously and "stiffened their necks." Perhaps

35

do you think is the "cure" for a stiff neck? What are some ways in which we rebel and try to live outside of God's law? How does God continue to deliver us?

❈ Paraphrase Nehemiah 9:16-17 in contemporary language. Read these aloud. How do the paraphrases help or hinder our understanding of the text?

Read a prayer of confession in a worship resource from your denomination. Look at some of your bulletins or orders of worship from past worship services. Identify prayers or acts of confession in each service. What do you think is the purpose of confession? What does the act of public confession do for us? Why confess in public instead of just privately? What benefits or detriments do you see in public confession?

"stiff necks" is an agricultural term for oxen that refused to submit to the yoke, implying stubborn impertinence. The writer compares God's people with work animals who refuse to obey. The people were not mindful of what God had done for them. They ignored the law of God and went their own way.

Verses 16 and 17a are a confession, but 17b declares how God forgave them and continued to deliver them. Even when the people made a golden calf to worship, when they left the law, God did not leave them. God provided manna and water. Their clothes did not wear out, and they were able to keep walking to possess the land. Verse 24 describes how God made it possible for them to possess the land. They did not acquire the land on their own by conquest and their own prowess, but through God. They went in and took possession of a rich land.

Then in 25b and 26 the confession begins again. The people became "fat," their blessing and prosperity turned into arrogance; and they "cast [God's] law behind their backs." The manna that was provided was always just enough and excess was not possible. When there was the possibility of excess, the people abused it.

The gesture of casting God's law behind the back evokes a careless tossing away of a great gift, leaving it in the dust. It is not recognizing the value of something priceless. The sinfulness of the people meant that their claim on the land was revoked, and they fell to their enemies. But God acted on behalf of the oppressed and in verse 27 delivered them from their suffering once again.

Humans, though created in the image of God, are flawed and have, according to Charles Wesley in one of his hymns, a "bent to sinning."[3] We have our own ways of stiffening our necks and casting God's law behind our backs. We think we can live our own way. In our fierce independence, we delude ourselves that we can make it on our own without God. Time and time again we ignore God and are not conscious of what God does for us. I, for one, have flippantly tossed aside my blessings or assumed that I just deserved them.

Write a group prayer of confession. Make a list of things you have done or not done as a group. Place these into a group prayer. Pray aloud the prayer of confession.

We continue to fashion our own idols to worship, which ultimately leads to suffering. We need to confess as God's people did, according to Nehemiah. We need to name our rebellions before God. Yet we often prefer to ignore confession, perhaps because we prefer to focus on God's forgiveness, perhaps because it forces us to face and admit our own failures and wrongdoing.

Christians everywhere affirm that we can confess to God in private prayer and receive God's forgiveness. It can also be a powerful experience to confess our shortcomings to one another in the faith community so that we may be accountable to

CLOSING TIME
Have a Hymn Sing.
Ask people to select hymns having to do with light, the light of God, or God's guidance. In what specific ways do the songs invite us to live in God's light?

Have a candlelight processional. Go into a darkened sanctuary. Carry Bibles, flashlights, or candles, and form a procession. Assign each person several Scripture verses to read aloud during the walk. Walk down the aisles of your sanctuary. Stop every few minutes to read the Scripture verses. End by coming together in a circle and praying. This may be done as an intergenerational activity.

❋ Pray a prayer of thanksgiving using the lists you created at the beginning of the session.

Sing "Thy Word Is a Lamp Unto My Feet," or play the song recorded by Amy Grant

and support one another. We also need to acknowledge the steadfastness and patience of God. Often, during a worship service, a prayer of confession is followed by words of assurance. In spite of our turning our backs, God continually saves us. God is being what God said God would be and do. The "I AM WHO I AM" is "slow to anger and abounding in steadfast love" (Nehemiah 9:17b).

CLOSING TIME

An African song has a catchy, repetitious line: "I am walking in the light of God." The text of Nehemiah reinforces that God is light, that God's word, God's commandments are a light for our path. Christians believe in, rely on, worship, and have a relationship with God. We affirm that God's word, which God has revealed to us through the Scripture, is true and right. We attempt to follow the way of God. Like the Hebrews, we, too, are a pilgrim people, on a journey with God, walking, walking, walking, in the light of God.

---

[1]Augustine, *Confessions*, edited by R. S. Pine-Coffin. London: Penguin Books, 1961, pages 263–67.

[2]*The Cloud of Unknowing*. New York: Paulist Press, 1981.

[3]Charles Wesley, "Love Divine, All Loves Excelling," *The United Methodist Hymnal*, 384.

INTERGENERATIONAL ACTIVITIES

Tell favorite family stories as described above, or have the candle-light processional, inviting all ages to participate.

Make shadow puppets. Use an old filmstrip or slide projector to project light onto a wall or screen. Appoint some adults to make shadow puppets with their hands, such as butterflies, snakes, trees, rabbits, giraffes. Have the children guess them. Talk about how shadows are created. Invite the children to practice their own shadow puppets or to perform in the spotlight.

Go on a Trust Walk. Pair adults with children or youth. Blindfold the adults and have the children lead them on a pre-selected route, either inside or outside the church. Explain that the person blindfolded has to trust the one leading, and the one leading has the responsibility to make sure the blindfolded one does not stumble or fall. Then switch roles on the return route. After the experience, talk about what it felt like to be the leader and what it felt like to be the one being led. Ask what it felt like not to be able to see where you are going. How easy it was to learn to trust your leader? Talk about how we trust God to guide us.

Chapter 3

*L*ight Among Us

Luke 1:28-38; 2:1-38

**GATHERING
MOMENTS**
❁ Greet one another.
Light a candle. Read
aloud John 12:34-36.
Ask: What does it
mean to you to be
"children of light"?

***Add either a star, pic-
ture of Jesus or an
angel to your display.***

❁ Read responsively
"A Litany of Light and
Darkness." Ponder the
phrase "even the
darkness is not dark
to you." What does
this mean? Talk about
how God is light to
you.

❁ Pray in unison the
"Opening Prayer."

***Write John 12:36 in
calligraphy.*** Obtain
inexpensive calligra-
phy pens from a craft

GATHERING MOMENTS

"Believe in the light, so that you may
become children of light." (John 12:36)

A LITANY OF LIGHT
AND DARKNESS

Leader: Justice is far from us, and right-
eousness does not reach us; we wait for
light, and lo! there is darkness; and for
brightness, but we walk in gloom.

*Group: The people who walked in darkness
have seen a great light; those who lived in a
land of deep darkness—on them light has
shined.*

Leader: We grope . . . like those who
have no eyes; we stumble at noon as in
the twilight, among the vigorous as
though we were dead.

*Group: The people who walked in darkness
have seen a great light; those who lived in a
land of deep darkness—on them light has
shined.*

store and a book that gives lettering instructions, or have a calligrapher demonstrate this art. Use these as tent cards for kitchen tables; or purchase small clear, plastic, stand-up frames.

PURPOSE
To understand that God's light came into the world in the person of Jesus and to explore ways we may live as children of the light.

THE SESSION PLAN
Choose from among the core teaching activities (identified with ❋). Add options in **bold italics** to extend beyond a 45- to-60-minute session.

SETTING THE SCENE
❋ Read Luke 1:28-38 aloud. What challenges you or makes you curious about Luke 1:28-38? What images or ideas impress you? In what way does this Scripture speak to you about hope?

Leader: If I say, "Surely the darkness shall cover me, and the light around me become night," even the darkness is not dark to you; the night is as bright as the day, for darkness is as light to you.

Group: The people who walked in darkness have seen a great light; those who lived in a land of deep darkness—on them light has shined.

All: This is the message we have heard from him and proclaim to you, that God is light and in him there is no darkness at all.

(Adapted from Isaiah 9:2; 59:9-10; Psalm 139:1-12; John 1:5)

AN OPENING PRAYER

God of light and love, you have given us a great light to shine in our darkness. Help us to let your light shine in all that we do. Help us to have the bright hope of eternal life; through Jesus Christ, the Light of the World. Amen.

SETTING THE SCENE

In John 12:34-36, Jesus uses the image of light as he invites the crowd to believe. The image of light carries the hope that all who believe may "shine" as the light of God shines in Jesus. Hope also shines in Luke 1:28-38 and 2:1-33. These passages from Luke tell three sto-

Take a "lounge chair" tour of the Holy Land. Obtain travel folders or brochures from travel agencies. Search the Internet for the Nazareth homepage or any other site that gives photos of modern-day Nazareth and the Church of the Annunciation. Project these where everyone can see, or gather around a computer to view the photos. Give brochures to participants.

ries about the birth of Jesus. Luke 1:28-38 tells about Gabriel's visit to Mary to announce the birth of Jesus. Luke 2:1-21 tells the story of the birth of Jesus and the visitation to the shepherds. Luke 2:22-38 describes the presentation of Jesus in the Temple and the responses of both Simeon and Anna. We will explore each of these as we focus on God's light among us in the person of Jesus.

We usually read these passages during the Christmas season. Reading them during a different time of year offers the opportunity to explore some of the lesser-known aspects of the stories and to plunge deeper into the meaning of the texts.

Tradition says that Luke was a physician and a companion or fellow worker of Paul and that Luke wrote both Luke and Acts. An ancient prologue to Luke's Gospel refers to the writer as a "Syrian of Antioch" who was a physician and a disciple of the apostles. Authorship of Luke, however, is subject to scholarly debate.

The writer of Luke's Gospel is a great storyteller. Each of the Gospels tells the story of Jesus in a different way. Matthew, Mark, and Luke are the Synoptic Gospels, which means "viewed together." These Gospels give a synopsis of Jesus' ministry, whereas the Gospel of John begins to present the meaning and effect of Jesus' teachings.

Scholars are uncertain about the exact date that the Gospel of Luke was written; however, they suggest the latter part of the first century A.D., probably during the 80's. In the first four verses of Luke, the writer acknowledges other sources and the desire to create "an orderly account." Not only is the "account" orderly, it is a purposeful and literary rendering of the life, ministry, crucifixion, and resurrection of Jesus that shows him as savior of all humankind.

The Gospel of Luke was written in a world ruled by Rome. One aspect of life under Roman rule was the palpable threat of persecution. Nero ruled as emperor of Rome from A.D. 54 to 68. In 64, during Nero's cruel and irresponsible reign, fire broke out in Rome. In order to divert suspicion from himself to another group, Nero blamed the Christians and began a systematic persecution. Later, under the reign of Emperor Trajan, a letter from Pliny, a Roman scholar, says that Christians who refused to worship the emperor should be killed.

Against this backdrop, the writer of Luke's Gospel presents Jesus as "a light for revelation" to Gentiles (all nations) and to Jews (Luke 2:32).

MARY AND GABRIEL
(LUKE 1:28-38)

MARY AND GABRIEL

❋ Review what happened in this encounter between Mary and Gabriel.

It is interesting that the Gospel of Luke features Mary in the birth announcement, whereas Matthew features Joseph. In the church year, the Annunciation is traditionally commemo-

43

Create a tabloid newspaper announcing this event. See *The Tabloid Bible,* by Nick Page, pages 109–114 (Westminster/John Knox Press, 1999) for examples. Discuss the headlines that the group decides to use. Do you agree or disagree with the view that the Incarnation is a scandal? Explain your view. Make copies of your tabloids, and hand them out to church-goers, to other Vacation Bible School participants, or to people on the streets.

Research Gabriel and angels. Look up *Gabriel* in a Bible dictionary. Another good resource is *Angels and Demons: What Do We Really Know About Them?* by Peter J. Kreeft (Ignatius Press, 1995).

rated on March 25. Since about the fourth century the church has observed the birth of John the Baptist as June 24 and of Jesus on December 25, about six months apart. These dates coincide with the summer and winter solstices. December 25 falls nine months after March 25, the day of the Annunciation.

The text tells us that the angel Gabriel was sent by God to Nazareth to a virgin who was engaged or betrothed to a man named Joseph. This event is known as the Annunciation, the announcement to Mary that she would bear the Messiah. Mary was very likely a young girl of about fifteen. The Church of the Annunciation, a beautiful shrine in Nazareth, commemorates this event. Nazareth, a good-size city now, was a village in Galilee at the time when Mary lived.

Mary was betrothed to Joseph, which was a more binding arrangement than a contemporary engagement. Betrothals were usually arranged by the bride's father, and the groom paid a "bride price." The bride continued to live in her father's house until the groom came and took her to live in his home. The wedding celebration lasted a week. Betrothal was a legally binding arrangement. Should the groom die before the wedding, the bride became a widow. The groom had to divorce the bride if he wished to get out of the arrangement.

Mary is a form of the name *Miriam,*

❋ Form teams of two or three. Assign the following Scriptures to each team, one Scripture to a team: Daniel 8:15-26; Daniel 9:21-27; and Luke 1:11-20. Discuss in each team: What does Gabriel do? What does the Scripture say to you about the function of angels? Report your discussions to the entire group.

Draw a picture of an angel. Give paper and markers to participants, and tell them to draw what they imagine an angel would look like. When they are done, invite them to tell about the pictures. Ask: What do you believe about angels? How do you think angels might function in the contemporary world? What experiences, if any, have you had with angels?

Moses' sister, a common Hebrew name that means, "perfect one." The visitation by an angel is one of many in the Bible, but perhaps this one is the most important and best loved. Angels were common in the belief system of first-century Jews. The word *angel* is the English translation of the Greek word *aggelos*, which means "messenger." The name *Gabriel* contains Hebrew words that mean "God" and "strength" or "man," and it suggests a variety of meanings that include "man of God," "God is my strength," or "God is my hero." Gabriel appears in both Luke 1:11-20 to announce the birth of John to Zechariah and Elizabeth and in the Old Testament, in Daniel 8:15-26 and 9:21-27.

This pronouncement by an angel of God follows a pattern similar to other birth announcements in the Bible. Gabriel has already made a similar announcement to Zechariah of John the Baptist's birth. Gabriel spoke enthusiastically to Mary, "Greetings, favored one!" Some ancient traditions also add "blessed are you among women." Then the angel attempted to calm Mary's fears with the words, "Do not be afraid." Gabriel told Mary that she would have a child and announced a name, which carried an identity in its meaning. "And you will name him Jesus," said Gabriel. The name *Jesus*, a Greek form of the name "Joshua," means "God saves" or "God Delivers." Gabriel described the future

45

Watch a clip from the movie, Michael, starring John Travolta. What does this film say about angels and our understanding of them? What are some of the characteristics of angels in general and this angel, in particular? What are some of our misconceptions about angels? How do you feel the film supports or denies the presence of angels in our midst? Why is or isn't this film a good way to learn about angels?

Using a concordance, find other references to the term *Son of God* in the Gospels, and look them up in your Bibles. Read these aloud. Find more information about this title for Jesus in a Bible dictionary. What is the role of the Son of God? What other titles are given for Jesus in the Bible?

role of this child as the "Son of the Most High," who would reign over the house of Jacob with a never-ending kingdom.

When told that she was to have a child, Mary asked, "How can this be, since I am a virgin?" Gabriel responded with the news of Elizabeth's pregnancy and the assurance that with God, nothing is impossible. Mary's response in Luke 1:38 echoes that of Hannah in 1 Samuel 1:18. Mary sang praises to God just as Hannah had done.

The tabloids in the grocery store check-out line announce a myriad of scandals about famous people in politics and entertainment, one paper trying to outdo the other with their announcements of who is having an extramarital affair, who is pregnant out of wedlock, or who is hooked on drugs. Such announcements are intended to shock the public, yet the public is somewhat numbed by the proliferation of such announcements. It takes a lot to shock us these days. For my money, the greatest scandal ever to occur in human history was God's decision, in the greatest act of love ever known, to enter our world in the person of Jesus. Why do I think about the Incarnation, or God taking human form, as a scandal? It is scandalous not so much because those around might have thought Mary was pregnant out of wedlock. It is scandalous because one is compelled to ask why would God, a God so great, good, pure, beautiful, and radiant,

46

willingly *choose* to enter such a dark and dismal world, a world so flawed and so broken? Why would God stoop so low? Because God loves us! It is as simple as that. God believes in us. Despite our brokenness, God believes we are still worthy of the light. God sent his only Son into the world that the whole world might be saved. The announcement of the angel Gabriel was an announcement of the greatest hope for the world.

THE BIRTH OF JESUS
❀ List all the sources of light or kinds of light that you can think of, such as electric light bulb, star, lighthouse. Beside each light source write a sentence on what contribution it makes to humankind, such as "helps us see" or "guides us to shore." Name each light source aloud followed by the sen-

THE BIRTH OF JESUS (LUKE 2:1-20)

Luke 2:1-20 is the beloved account of Jesus' birth, how the light of God came to be among us. Emperor Augustus reigned from 27 B.C. to A.D. 14. Governments in biblical times kept track of people by taking a census, much as we do today. Sometimes these registrations were used to tax and oppress people. However, no record of a census of "all the world," during the reign of Augustus exists. Quirinius was a military advisor of

Son of God

Gabriel tells Mary that the child born to her will be called the "Son of God." This term, used in Luke 1:35, occurs only six times in Luke. John's Gospel uses it more often. It is used as an analogy to define Jesus' relationship to God as a son to a father, a very close relationship in Hebrew culture.

tence about its contribution. Then replace the name of the light source with the word *Jesus* and read each sentence again. What feelings or thoughts occur to you?

Continue the lounge chair tour. Locate a Web site for Bethlehem. Look for pictures of the Church of the Nativity. Or, have someone who has been to the Holy Land describe his or her experience and show pictures.

Collect and bring in pictures of Jesus at various ages. You may find some on the Internet or in your church. Display these. What do you notice about these pictures? What feelings or thoughts do they evoke for you? How do the artists use light?

LET US GO NOW
❁ Make copies of Luke 2:8-20 for each person. Tell group members to try to see, hear, smell, taste, and feel the elements of

Augustus. In A.D. 6, Quirinius became the governor of Syria; and he did do a census of Judea.

David had captured the territory around Bethlehem, five miles south of Jerusalem and made it his home. Joseph was one of David's descendants. The site of Jesus' birth was very likely a cave, many of which were used as stables in the hill country surrounding Jerusalem. Today, the Church of the Nativity, first erected by Helena, mother of Constantine in A.D. 330 and then replaced by the Emperor Justinian around 565, stands at the spot traditionally identified as the birthplace of Jesus. A silver star of David marks the designated spot. Until recent unrest, pilgrims came daily to touch the star and pray.

"LET US GO NOW . . . AND SEE"

When our daughter was about three years old, my husband and I went Christmas shopping on that dreaded Friday after Thanksgiving, taking her with us. We must have been out of our minds. You could not get within two miles of the mall. I confess that I like to shop. My husband, on the other hand, would rather chew nails. The mall was filled with plastic tinsel and piped-in Christmas music. After a full day of "shop till you drop" with a cranky three-year-old, we finally left the mall. Tired, hungry, and irritable, all three of us the story while re-reading this passage. Spend time in the fields with the shepherds. What did they see and hear? What is the "glory of the Lord"? Experience their joy, and tell about times that you have been joyful upon hearing the word of the Lord. When have you known the glory of the Lord? Write in your journals about this experience.

walked the long hike to the car. I knew I had succumbed to the worst kind of commercialism. On the way home, my husband and I began to argue about money.

"Stop!" my daughter shouted. "Stop the car! I want to see Jesus."

"What?" I asked.

"Look over there," she pointed.

We had passed a church with one of those Nativity scenes in the front yard.

"I want to see that Jesus," my daughter repeated.

What a cranky three-year-old wants, she usually gets. My husband stopped the car. Without saying a word, we got out and walked up to the Nativity scene in the churchyard. We stared down at the baby Jesus in Mary's lap. After a time, we knelt down and held hands.

"There. There is Jesus," I said.

"Yes," said my daughter, at last satisfied.

Today when I remember that day, I think of the old hymn,

> Turn your eyes upon Jesus,
>   look full in his wonderful face,
> and the things of the earth will grow
>   strangely dim
>   in the light of his glory and grace.

When we looked upon Jesus, all the tinsel and fake Christmas trees, all the arguing, all the frenzy faded away. All that remained was "the light of his glory and grace."

After the birth of Jesus, the story takes

❀ Locate the Christmas carol, "While Shepherds Watched Their Flocks," in a hymn-book. Read or sing the words.

the reader to the fields where the shepherds were doing what they normally do, watching their sheep. We imagine a beautiful, cool starry night. Suddenly an angel appeared in the sky. The text says, "the glory of the Lord shone around them." Then we note that a host of angels joined the one who brought the news. We imagine light, perhaps an aura, glowing in the night; and we sense the shepherds' fear. The shepherds were compelled to go to Bethlehem to see the child. As they told their story, all were amazed, including Mary who "pondered these things in her heart." As the shepherds returned to their duties they glorified and praised God. God's message was true. They had seen the Holy Child, and what they saw brought them joy. Though their lives may have gone on much the same outwardly, we imagine that inwardly the shepherds were changed forever.

SIMEON PRESENTS JESUS
❀ Read Luke 2:20-38 aloud. What images or ideas in this story stand out for you? Why?

SIMEON PRESENTS JESUS (LUKE 2:21-38)

When it came time for Jesus' circumcision according to the law of Moses, his parents took him to the Temple in Jerusalem. Circumcision was a ritual of the child's acceptance into the community. In Luke's account, the emphasis falls upon the name given by the angel. Luke's description of the presentation of Jesus in the Temple also includes ele-

Continue the lounge chair tour by looking at the Jerusalem homepage. The Web site gives some photos, information, and research on the Temple location. Or, look at a diagram of the Temple in Bible reference books. Close your eyes and walk through the encounter of Simeon, Anna, and the Holy Family in your mind.

❃ *Look up* Simeon *and* Anna *in a Bible dictionary.* How do you see the roles of Simeon and Anna in Luke's narrative? How do you think they knew that Jesus was the Messiah? What do you think it means to say that Jesus is a light for revelation to the Gentiles and glory to

ments that suggest both the redemption of the firstborn child and the purification rites of the mother who was considered to be unclean after childbirth. The offering of "a pair of turtledoves or two young pigeons" indicated that the couple could not afford to offer a lamb and a turtledove or pigeon. Their offering was the offering of the poor. According to the story told in Luke, Simeon, a "righteous and devout" man who had been told by the Lord that he would not die until he had seen the Messiah, blessed the infant Jesus. The name *Simeon* means, "God hears."

Simeon had waited patiently, never doubting that the Messiah would come. The Scripture says that the Holy Spirit guided Simeon to the Temple and that he was present when the family arrived.

Simeon saw the child as Mary and Joseph brought him into the Temple, then he took the child in his arms and praised God.

What Simeon said has become one of the great hymns of the church. These words are known as the *Nunc Dimittis* from the first words of the Latin translation for "now you are dismissing." The Nunc Dimittis is the last of four hymns in the infancy narrative of Luke's Gospel. The other three are the Magnificat (Luke 1:46-55), the Benedictus (Luke 1:68-79), and the hymn of the heavenly host (Luke 2:14). When Simeon blessed the child, he called him a mighty savior who will be "a light for

God's people Israel?

⦿ Look up Isaiah 40:5; 42:6; 46:13; 49:6; and 52:9-10. Read each Scripture aloud. Why do you think the Gospel writers believed that Jesus fulfilled these Hebrew Scriptures? How do you think Jesus fulfills these Scriptures today? Write responses to these questions in your journal. Tell about your responses in the group.

LIGHT IN THE WORLD
⦿ Read aloud John 1:1-18. How does the true light contrast with false lights? What are some of those false lights we experience today? How do they mislead us? How has Christ given light to direct your life?

Bring light into someone else's world. Continue the mission project that you selected in the first session. Another way to bring light into someone else's world might be to hold a

revelation to the Gentiles and for glory to [God's] people Israel." All three of these themes echo the prophet Isaiah (40:5; 42:6; 46:13; 49:6; 52:9-10).

Anna, an elderly widow and a prophet, a model of the good and pious widow of the Jews and of the early church, never left the Temple. She worshiped there night and day with prayer and fasting. Anna, too, is said to praise God, although her hymn is not included in Luke's story. Luke does say that she told all "who were looking for the redemption of Jerusalem" about the child.

LIGHT IN THE WORLD

A beautiful stained glass window in the National Cathedral in Washington, DC, depicts the scene in which the heavenly host appears to the shepherds. Although it is a small window, it gives the illusion of expansive fields covered with sheep. With the sunlight behind the window, the hues of blue and green are brilliant. The "glory of the Lord" is clearly evident. One would think the artist had been physically present on the night of Jesus' birth.

According to the Gospel of John "the true light, which enlightens everyone, was coming into the world" (John 1:9). Jesus was and is truly light among us, and one of the ways we celebrate the Light of the World is with Christmas lights. Many people have a tradition of driving around sing-along in an assisted living facility for people with Alzheimer's disease.

CLOSING TIME
Read aloud the poem, "Star-Giving," by Ann Weems. When have you been given a "star" by God?

❀ Sing the hymn, "I Want to Walk as a Child of the Light." What do you think it means to live as a child of the light?

❀ Close by reading aloud the *Nunc Dimittus* (Luke 2:29-32).

after church on Christmas Eve to view the extravagant displays.

False lights that appear to light the way abound in our world, but these lights quickly fade. The light of Christ overcomes the darkness and lights the way for every one of us.

CLOSING TIME

John 12:36 urges readers to believe in the light in order to become children of light. Jesus illuminates that potential for all humans in all ages.

In her poem, "Star-Giving," Ann Weems wrote about the desire to give a star as a Christmas gift. After listing several ways the star would serve the one who received it, Weems says:

> *But Stars are only God's for giving,*
> *And I must be content to give you words and*
> > *wishes*
> > > —*Reaching for Rainbows,*
> > > Westminster Press, 1980; page 72

INTERGENERATIONAL ACTIVITIES

Go outside; look up at the night sky. Talk about what the sky might have looked like the night the angels appeared to the shepherds.

Build a campfire and roleplay what the shepherds might have said about what they saw. If you are inside, make an artificial campfire using wooden logs and red, orange, and yellow strips of construction paper cut in the shape of flames. Use this artificial campfire as a gathering place to tell shepherd stories.

Have an impromptu, summer-time Christmas pageant. Have the children be sheep or shepherds. Give everyone a part. Read the text from Luke slowly and have the actors pantomime the story. Include Simeon and Anna in the Temple. Sing Christmas carols.

Make a diorama. Turn a medium-size moving box on its side. Cut off the flaps so the side is open. Cover the inside on three sides with dark blue or black construction paper. Place brown construction paper on the bottom. Add some rocks and grass for effect. Have the children make sheep from cotton balls, and cut out stand-up shepherds from cardboard or old file folders. Then there are two alternatives. Either punch little holes all over the sides of the box (through the paper also) and insert the bulbs of a string of white Christmas lights. Plug in the lights and turn out other lights to view the diorama. Or, you may cut a hole in the top of the box and insert a black light. Turn off all the lights and view the diorama.

If you have stained glass windows in your church, have someone talk to the group about them. Tell the stories that the windows represent. Give a stained glass window tour at your own church or at another church nearby. Or, have a stained glass artist visit to talk about how a stained glass window is created. Talk about how important light is to the effect and beauty of stained glass. Why do stained glass windows adorn many of our churches, old and modern? Research and tell about how this art form developed in the history of the church.

Make stained glass candleholders. Purchase tea candles (one for each person) and small jars or glasses large enough to hold the candles. Purchase a bag of broken colored glass, available at most craft stores. Add water to plaster of Paris, and cover each jar with the mixture. While wearing gloves, press bits of colored glass into it. Cover the entire jar. Allow this to dry before inserting and lighting the candle. Talk about the effects of light on the glass. How is light an important symbol for Christ?

Chapter 4

*T*he Light of the World

John 3:1-21; 8:12; 12:35-36; Matthew 5:14-16

**GATHERING
MOMENTS**

✸ By candlelight or
the light of an oil
lantern read respon-
sively "A Litany of
Light and Darkness."
Remain silent for a
moment.

**Add a globe and
cross to your display**
to represent Christ as
the light of the world.

✸ Sing the hymn, "To
God Be the Glory."

*Look up the life story
of hymn writer Fanny
J. Crosby.* Fanny J.
Crosby: An
Autobiography (Wipf
& Stock Publishers,
1999). What does her
life say to you about
living in God's light?

GATHERING MOMENTS

To God Be the Glory

"To God be the glory!"

This hymn tells the gospel story: God loved the world and gave his Son that the world might have life. Fanny J. Crosby, who was blind, wrote the hymn in 1875. She offered it in praise of God's activity and life in spite of her blindness. The word *glory* is especially poignant because it suggests both praise and light. In her darkness, Fanny Crosby offered light and praise to God and invites those who sing it to do the same.

A LITANY OF LIGHT AND DARKNESS

For once we were in darkness, but now we are in the light.
Help us to live as children of light.

For God so loved the world that he gave his only Son, so that everyone who

55

PURPOSE
To explore the encounter between Jesus and Nicodemus in order to consider how refusing or accepting God's light in Christ might affect daily life.

THE SESSION PLAN
Choose from among the core teaching activities (identified with ❀). Add options in **bold italics** to extend beyond a 45-to-60-minute session.

SETTING THE SCENE
❀ Read aloud John 3:1-21. Write a paraphrase of the dialogue between Jesus and Nicodemus in contemporary language. Pair up and act out this encounter before the large group using the paraphrases.

Conduct a character analysis of Nicodemus. List all of his positive and negative characteristics. Discuss these. Have you tried to persuade someone of something, but that person just did not "get it"? Did you feel you

believes in him may not perish but may have eternal life.
Help us to live as children of light.

For once we were in darkness, but now we are in the light.
Help us to live as children of light.

SETTING THE SCENE

The encounter between Jesus and Nicodemus occurs only in John's Gospel. John is called "the spiritual gospel" because unlike Matthew, Mark, and Luke, which present similar synopses of Jesus' life and ministry, John selects specific material that will contribute to the main concern: Jesus is the incarnate Word of God who became flesh and lived among us. The encounter between Jesus and Nicodemus offers possibility for human life. A human being can be born of flesh and of the Spirit.

The Scripture for this session contains John 3:16, which Martin Luther called the "gospel in miniature." Jesus, the only Son of God, came that the world might have life. The Greek word that is translated "only Son" in the New Revised Standard Version is *monogenes*, which combines *mono* ("only") and a form of *ginomai* ("to cause to be"). The King James Version translates this word as "begotten." The Word of God, uniquely "begotten," "caused to be," or "generated" by God, "became flesh and lived were "talking past each other"? Who do you think are the "Nicodemuses" of today?

Practice Lectio Divina. Choose either John 8:12, John 12:36, or Matthew 5:14-16. Go through the four stages listed below. Allow twenty minutes for this exercise.

Lectio
Read the text slowly. What does the text say?
Read it again. Listen to the text.

Meditatio
Repeat a phrase that "lights up" or "rings a bell" for you.
Listen for what God is saying to you through this text.
Think about what the text means.

Oratio
Respond to the divine presence. How will you live it out?
Pray your response to the Word.

Contemplatio
Rest at the place it leads you.
Be with God.

among us" (John 1:14). In the Gospel of John, God gave the Word to us in Jesus that we may have life.

This passage has two parts: the dialogue between Jesus and Nicodemus (3:1-10), followed by a discourse, a lengthy discussion or teaching, given by Jesus (3:11-21). This pattern—dialogue followed by discourse—is a common pattern in John's Gospel. Nicodemus is identified as a Pharisee, a "ruler of the Jews" and "teacher of Israel" (verse 10). These are high credentials. Perhaps Nicodemus was a member of the Sanhedrin, the Jewish high council of seventy. Pharisees were an important group in Judea. They were learned, laypeople who were experts in the laws and who were concerned with righteous living. Some of them are depicted as being very suspicious of Jesus. Many expected that the promised Messiah would perform signs and miracles (John 2:23).

John 3:19-21; 8:12; and 12:35-36 highlight Jesus as the light of the world. The Gospel tells the reader that some people prefer to walk in darkness and "hate the light" (3:20). John urges readers to believe in the light and to live as children of the light (12:35-36). The light of God shines through Jesus, the "only begotten" of God. A person who chooses to live in the light becomes a child of the light. The image of light unifies the believer with God through Jesus, and the

Reflect on your experience with *lectio divina*. What words or phrases from your text struck you? What insights did you gain? How is praying with the Scriptures different from studying them? Choose one image from your passage, and write your thoughts on it in your journal.

NIGHT VISITOR
In small groups look up kingdom of God *in Bible reference books*. Find out as much as you can about the meaning of this term. Write the information you find on a large sheet of paper. Relay this to the whole group. How is the kingdom of God both now and in the future? What does it mean to see the kingdom of God?

believer becomes a way for others to see God's light. The believer does not "generate" the light. God generates the light, gives the light through Jesus, and through Jesus offers life-giving light to believers.

Matthew 5:14-16 uses light imagery in a different way. The Scripture, included in the collection of teachings called the Sermon on the Mount, uses the image of light to describe the listeners. Jesus called the people the light of the world and urged them to let their lights shine in order that others might see their good works and give glory to God.

NIGHT VISITOR

Nicodemus came to Jesus in the night. Maybe he was sneaking around so that no one would see him, and he may have wished to avoid ridicule or criticism from other Pharisees. African American slaves saw in this nighttime visit a model of courage. A person could come to Jesus at night even when those who were in power were against it. Slaves were forbidden to come together for worship, and many gathered clandestinely at night.[1] Or, perhaps nighttime allowed conversation without the noise and distraction of a crowd. It was not unusual to stay up late and discuss the law. Nicodemus does seem to be "in the dark" about who Jesus is and what he is about.

In John's Gospel, Nicodemus

58

❀ Read the baptism ritual in your church's worship resources. What is the purpose of the ritual? Discuss the meaning of baptism and the role it plays in the new birth. Discuss the imagery about dying and rising with Christ. What is the role of water and the Spirit? What does it mean to be born again? How do you understand the meaning of "born from above"? Pass a basin filled with water to each group membere, then pass a towel. Dip your hands in the water and say, one by one, "We remember our baptism with thanksgiving." Dry your hands with the towel.

Create two group collages. Label the first one "Birth"; look for pictures in magazines about birth. Glue these on a large sheet of butcher paper (or any large sheet of paper). Label the second one "New Birth"; look for words or pictures that describe what it means to be

addressed Jesus as "Rabbi," a term of respect. He began with a statement, perhaps a ruse. "Rabbi, we know that you are a teacher who has come from God; for no one can do these signs that you do apart from the presence of God" (3:2). Jesus answers him with "Very truly, I tell you," which is a phrase that introduces a new teaching. "No one can see the kingdom of God without being born from above," Jesus states. The answer seems strange and unrelated at first.

The writer of John often used words with double meanings as a literary device. The phrase in Greek is *gennao anothen*, which means more than a second birth. Life is generated or caused to be born from "above," "again," or "anew." The tapestry of meaning is lost in the English translation because there are no equivalent English words. Nicodemus took Jesus literally and said that it is physiologically impossible to be born twice. You cannot go back into your mother's womb.

Jesus tried again to get through to Nicodemus: "No one can enter the kingdom of God without being born of water and the Spirit." Jesus contrasted flesh and spirit, and he announced that the kingdom of God can be entered by those who are born from above. For Jesus, the kingdom of God was something more than vanquishing Rome and restoring the glory of the ancient Jerusalem as it was in the reign of King David.

born from above. Glue these pictures on another large sheet of paper. Discuss the contrast between the two terms. Display these collages. Talk about the experience of the new birth and what this is like.

Obtain a copy of John Wesley's sermon, "The New Birth." The text of this sermon may be found in *The Works of John Wesley, Sermons* (Vol. 2, edited by Albert Outler) or on the World Wide Web at www.biblestudyhelps.com. Click on "Sermons." Click on "Wesley," then click on "sermon 45." Divide into small groups and assign different parts of the sermon to each group. Ask each group to analyze its part of Wesley's message and explain it to the whole group.

Using a concordance, find other references to the term Son of Man in the Bible. Locate these and read

The allusion to water and Spirit may hint at baptism, the church's re-enactment of Jesus' promise of new birth, although scholars disagree on this point. In the birthing process, the breaking of the waters of birth signals the impending birth of a baby. To be born of water *and* the Spirit is another kind of birth. It is a dying to one's old life and a rising with Christ to a new life. Water symbolizes cleansing and refreshment. The Spirit gives the new life that comes from knowing God. To be born of water and the Spirit means to receive God's cleansing grace. Nicodemus would have been familiar with Jewish rites of purification with water; however, "to be born of water and the Spirit" was not simply an outward ritual but an inward acceptance of God's grace. "Born Again" is not just a slogan or a designation for some special kind of Christian. To be born again or born from above is to enter into new life, a life generated by God.

In verse 8, Jesus talks about the wind. The Greek word, *pneuma*, carries a constellation of meanings that include breath, spirit, and vital principle, all of which are similar to the meanings of the Hebrew word *ruah*. Jesus offers the wind as a way of explaining "born from above." Wind "blows where it chooses" and a person does not know "where it comes from or where it goes." The enigmatic explanation using a word that suggests multiple levels of meaning is the mystery offered by Jesus. Nicodemus them aloud. Find more information about this title for Jesus in a Bible dictionary. What is the role of the Son of Man? Why does Jesus stress that he ascended and descended from heaven? Compare and contrast this term with *Son of God.*

❀ Write a short story about what might have happened to Nicodemus after his encounter with Jesus. Use imagination and humor. Read your stories aloud and discuss them.

answered incredulously, "How can these things be?" His preconceived notions were a barrier to his receiving and understanding Jesus.

Nicodemus's lack of understanding makes him a representative of all who do not understand and, therefore, reject the teachings of Jesus. The failure to connect does, however, provide an opportunity for the Fourth Evangelist to proclaim the good news:

> For God so loved the world that he gave
> his only Son, so that everyone
> who believes in him may not perish
> but have eternal life. (3:16)

Nicodemus reappears in John 7:50 and 19:39. We are told that he defended Jesus to the chief priest and joined with Joseph of Arimathea in preparing Jesus' body for burial. The Gospel does not tell us whether Nicodemus became a believer.

Son of Man

- Jesus' self-designation in John 1:51
- Derived from a Hebrew and Aramaic idiom for human being
- Associated with heavenly ascent and descent
- Implies "privileged access to God"[2]
- A healing agent
- Divine who became human
- Used 93 times in Ezekiel
- Apocalyptic figure (see Daniel 7:13; Matthew 25:31; Acts 7:56)

**LIGHT
OF THE WORLD**
⚘ Read other "I AM"
Scriptures. Look up
John 6:35; 6:51;
10:7-9; 11:25-26;
14:6; 15:1. What do
these say about
Christ? How do you
think these sayings
relate to the "I AM"
statement in Exodus
3:14?

Write a prayer.
Make a list of the
images in the "I AM"
sayings listed above.
Work as a group, and
use these images to
create a prayer. Pray
the group prayer
aloud.

LIGHT OF THE WORLD

In John 8:12, Jesus declared himself to be the light of the world. This passage is one of the "I am" statements of Jesus found throughout John. The context for this statement is the Festival of Tabernacles or Booths, which provided the opportunity for the analogy. Risking arrest, Jesus went to the Temple during the middle of the festival and began to teach (7:14). At the end of the first day of the festival, four large lamps were lit in the Court of Women in the Temple. People sang and danced before the large lamps. As they celebrated, they held torches, which added to the light. The light commemorated how God led the people out of the wilderness by fire (Exodus 13:21). The celebration and the accompanying light imagery connect Jesus' "I am" statement with the experience of Moses in Exodus 3:14.

We take light for granted today in a way people did not in Jesus' day. Light was provided during the darkness of night by burning oil lamps or wood. Light in the darkness was a powerful image for God.

To this day I can hear my post-Depression–generation father to this day admonishing his children to turn out lights when leaving a room. "What? You think electricity grows on trees?" Nowadays we hardly worry about having enough light. We have very little compunction about leaving lights on. In fact, one motel chain advertises, "We'll leave the light on for you." Yet, if we think about the availability and brilliance of light in the contemporary world, the image of light continues to offer a vital way to think about God's presence in our world.

HATING THE LIGHT

HATING THE LIGHT

❋ Explore news stories. Look at recent events in newspapers or news magazines. Identify elements in the stories that demonstrate what it means to "hate the light." What do you think would be different in the story if those involved loved the light?

Scripture abounds with light imagery: the Creation (Genesis 1:3-4), the burning bush (Exodus 3), the pillar of fire (Exodus 13:21), the Word of God or Law (Psalm 119:105). The Gospel of John associates light with the Word of God in Jesus who became flesh. Yet, John 3:19-20 says, "The light has come into the world, and people loved darkness rather than light because their deeds were evil. For all who do evil hate the light."

Light reveals, and sometimes we don't want to see. We act in some ways like ants that live under a rock. When the rock is turned over, the ants scurry everywhere as they try to get out of the light. They want to be hidden. We, too, hide in the darkness. Politicians sometimes duck questions about or lie about moral failings when they are exposed. Clergy accused of sexual misconduct are sometimes sheltered by the church. Alcoholics sometimes drink in secret. We hide in darkness. We do not want others to see; and quite often, we do not wish to see.

People who surrounded Jesus

63

demanded miracles, "signs" as John called them, as a condition for believing. Yet, even though Jesus did perform extraordinary miracles, many still rejected him. People look at the light from afar and try to understand it; but they get so used to the darkness, so comfortable with it, that they are afraid of the light. Nicodemus tried to understand the meaning of the light, but it was difficult for him to go outside his own categories of understanding.

We sometimes want easy answers, as Nicodemus did. We want to accept the light on our own terms. We want to make God into what we think God ought to be. If God will not be as we think God *ought* to be, we ask along with Nicodemus, "How can these things be?" (3:9). We risk rejecting the light of God's truth. It is too difficult to go outside our own categories of understanding (John 3:9).

ELUSIVE LIGHT
☸ Create a mural. Brainstorm properties of light. Illustrate examples of these properties on a long sheet of paper. How is God's light elusive for you? What does the light of Christ reveal to you about God? How might your actions reveal something about the light of Christ to the world?

ELUSIVE LIGHT

The light of our world eludes definition. Scientists have explored the properties of light for centuries but have not yet completely defined light. Ancient Greeks believed that light consisted of a stream of particles. Isaac Newton supported this theory. In the 1800's, Thomas Young conducted experiments that showed that light behaved like a wave. In 1887, Maxwell's theory of light as electromagnetic energy was confirmed.

Theories of Light

- Newton's theory—light consists of particles called *corpuscles*; this theory only explained reflection
- Wave theory of light (Maxwell's theory)—light behaves like a wave; this explained all the properties of light such as reflection, refraction, diffraction, and interference; it did not explain the photoelectric effect or radiation produced by an incandescent light
- Quantum theory (Einstein's theory)—light has a dual nature; when light is transmitted through space or matter, it behaves like a wave; when light is emitted or absorbed, it behaves like a particle called a *photon*

Albert Einstein won a Nobel Prize in 1921 for the theory that light consists of discrete particles or bundles of energy called photons.

Very hot objects, such as stars, generate so much energy that they give off many forms of electromagnetic energy, including light. Light bulbs generate visible light by converting electrical energy into light energy. Some chemical reactions produce light. Light can also be a stimulus. Some chemicals need light to react with other chemicals. A plant uses light energy for photosynthesis to take place, making food for the plant. The light energy also reacts with the rods and cones of the retina of our eyes, which causes us to see color.

The science of light in our world is fascinating; but thus far, it has only defined how light behaves. The full nature of light eludes human knowledge. Science does, however, offer an analogy for the way the human mind seeks to describe the Light of the World. We cannot fully know God, yet we can glimpse something of the nature of God as we look at Jesus, describe his teachings and actions, and ask ourselves how they inform life and action in our daily lives. Through Jesus, we can be children of light without fully understanding the Light.

LOVING DARKNESS

LOVING DARKNESS
❋ Read the poem "Loving Darkness." What does the poem say to you about darkness? about light? What does the last stanza say to you?

Loving Darkness

Ones who have loved darkness
more than light
shake their heads from side to side
in a quandary.

Try to unpack
and pull apart,
unravel each layer
to understand how light works,
only that
cannot be understood.

Nothing to do
but walk away,
walk away from love
in the dark.
Been there, done that.
Loved darkness
more than light,
with blue fire passion.

She brought it all
into the light.
And watched it burn away.

Now she goes around,
Edges singed with glory,
Singing of the Light.

—Susan Willhauck

An interesting paradox is that darkness can be an opportunity that propels us into the light. Saint John of the Cross wrote *Dark Night of the Soul.* It was in this hour of darkness that he found Christ. So alcoholics, politicians, fallen clergy, indeed any of us can come to the light, no questions asked.

Joyce Rupp in *Little Pieces of Light . . . : Darkness and Personal Growth* (Paulist Press, 1995) gives encouragement to those who seem trapped in darkness. She suggests that entering personal darkness, in other words looking at emotions and memories that cause pain or guilt, can help a person grow.

Throughout history good people have had to live in secret and move in darkness to protect themselves and to promote what they stood for. Early Christians had to worship in secret. So did African American slaves. The underground railroad and the underground resistance to the Nazis operated for justice during the night. In the mindset of John's Gospel, these forms of darkness are light.

LET YOUR LIGHT SHINE!

In the Gospel of Matthew, Jesus refers to believers as the "light of the world."

Write in your journal about those who love the darkness. Describe times when you have loved darkness more than light. What made you come into the light?

LET YOUR LIGHT SHINE!
Commit to telling about or showing the

light of Christ to someone tomorrow or in-between sessions. Talk about and give some examples of how you might do this. For example, how might you let your light shine to a neighbor that you do not know very well? Report on this experience at the final session.

Create bookmarks. Find pictures of a variety of sources of light. Select one that especially appeals to you. Cut it out and glue it onto a 2-inch by 6-inch strip of cardboard. Write "Let It Shine!" on the bookmark to remind you of your commitment to let the light of Christ shine through you.

CLOSING TIME
❁ Sing "This Little Light of Mine."

Now that you have light, let it shine, he says: Give it away. Psalm 105 instructs us to "Sing to him, sing praises to him; / tell of all his wonderful works" (verse 2).

The Gospel of Matthew seems to acknowledge that sometimes people who come to believe, who receive the light, hide it. We do not want to be too pushy or force our beliefs on others. Do we hide our lamp under a bushel? Why go to the trouble of lighting the lamp if we are going to hide it? Would others know that we are Christians by the way we live our lives? "Let your light shine before others, so that they may see your good works and give glory to your Father in heaven," writes Matthew (5:16). Jesus wants believers to witness to others in word and deed, to influence the world.

A former chef from New York who uses his talents to cook for a church-run homeless shelter said in an interview, "I have a hard time talking to others about my faith, so I cook to show my faith." As a friend always ends his e-mails to me, "Shine on!"

CLOSING TIME

A childhood song says, "This little light of mine, I'm gonna let it shine." It builds upon the words of Jesus in Matthew 5:14-16 and calls every believer to engage with the world. The most basic and recognizable attribute of light is to shine.

68

For once you were in darkness,
but now in the Lord you are light.
Live as children of light
—Ephesians 5:8

❋ Close by reading
Ephesians 5:8 and "A
Prayer for Light"
aloud.

A PRAYER FOR LIGHT

Let us pray:
O God, great giver of light,
Source of all brightness,
illumine us this day.
Reveal to us our misdeeds,
be a clear light to guide our way,
that we might bring your light to others.
Amen.

---

[1]*The New Interpreter's Bible,* Volume IX:
Abingdon Press, 1995; page 555.
[2]Ibid., page 551.

INTERGENERATIONAL ACTIVITIES

Have a dance of lights. Ask everyone to bring a flashlight. Go to a darkened room or outside, if it is night. Play folk music. Dance to the music while waving the flashlights. Afterward, talk about the importance of light and the joy that light brings.

Recreate the roleplay of the paraphrases of the Jesus/Nicodemus encounter for the whole Vacation Bible School (See "Setting the Scene," page 56).

Hold a candlelight dinner at a homeless shelter. Use candelabra and white tablecloths. Cook and serve a well-balanced, delicious meal. Read John 8:12 and Matthew 5:14-16 aloud, and talk with those present about Christ.

Encourage the light. Tell stories of the ways members of your congregation quietly give God's light to others. Invite those persons to be present while another person tells their story. Invite them to respond.

Draw pictures of ways we can let God's light shine through us. Show these and tell about them. Create a bulletin board using these pictures with the heading, "Letting Our Light Shine."

Chapter 5

$\mathcal{I}$ Saw the Light

Acts 9:1-20

GATHERING MOMENTS

✿ Go to the sanctu-·ary or to a worship center in the learning area. Pray Isaiah 9:2 and Psalm 43:3-5 aloud. Spend a few moments in silent prayer.

Add sunglasses or a suitcase to your display.

Sing** "**I Saw the Light**," **or listen to a recording of this song. A bluegrass version may be found on Bill Monroe's CD entitled, *The Best of Bill Monroe: The Millennium Collection*, 20th Century Masters series. Talk about the words to this song and what story they tell.

GATHERING MOMENTS

The people who walked in darkness
    have seen a great light;
those who lived in a land of deep
        darkness—
    on them light has shined.
                —Isaiah 9:2

O send out your light and your truth;
    let them lead me;
let them bring me to your holy hill
    and to your dwelling.
Then I will go to the altar of God,
    to God my exceeding joy;
and I will praise you with the harp,
    O God, my God.
Why are you cast down, O my soul,
    and why are you disquieted within
    me?
Hope in God; for I shall again praise him,
    my help and my God.
              —Psalm 43:3-5

The gospel hymn "I Saw the Light" celebrates a conversion experience. "I saw the light," it says. For the singer there is no more darkness or night. The experience has erased sorrow, and the singer is happy.

The liveliness of the song and the metaphor of light captures the joy of the conversion experience.

AN OPENING PRAYER

God of life and light, help us to see you. Help us to know the joy of your life-transforming love as we walk the paths of our lives; in Christ, we pray. Amen.

SETTING THE SCENE

Acts 9:1-20 is perhaps the most famous conversion story ever told. It is the story of a call and of Saul's surrender to Jesus. In the Book of Acts this story follows the stories of the conversion of the Samaritans and of the Ethiopian official. We first meet Saul in Acts 7:58 where he is identified as a "young man" who watched over the garments of those who stoned Stephen. Stephen went courageously to his death and in his final speech admonished the "stiff-necked people" (7:51) who refused the Holy Spirit. *Stiff-necked* is the same term used in Nehemiah 9:16.

Saul is a Pharisee from Tarsus, capital of the Roman province of Cilicia, which was located in what is now Turkey. Tarsus was a center for tent-making,

SETTING THE SCENE
❁ Read or tell the story from Acts 9:1-20. What, if anything, about the Scripture challenges you? What makes you want to know more?

Recreate Saul's experience on the road to Damascus. Go as a class to a road near your church and re-enact Saul's conversion experience. Have one group member read the Scripture as others mime the actions.

❁ Begin to construct "Before" and "After"

pictures of Saul, which you will work on as the session unfolds. Cut out two large silhouettes of a man from newsprint or other lightweight paper. You can have someone lie down on the paper to use as a pattern. Hang both of these on your class-room wall. Label them "Before" and "After." Begin to write words that describe Saul before his con-version on the "Before" picture.

Read the accounts of the Samaritan's and the Ethiopian's con-versions in Acts 8:9-13 and 8:26-40. How are their conversions like Saul's? How do they differ?

Find out more about "The Way" as an early designation for followers of Christ. Look up this term in Bible reference books. What does it say to you about those who believed in Jesus?

which was Saul's profession. Saul perse-cuted Christians in Jerusalem, and he wanted to go to Damascus to look for Christians. Chapter 9 tells of Saul's unre-lenting search for followers of "The Way" and how he dragged them from their homes and sent them to jail. "The Way" is believed to be the earliest self-designation for the followers of Jesus, in other words, the first name of the church, a name that suggests practice as well as belief.

Saul's conversion experience occurred on the road from Jerusalem to Damascus, which was about a week's journey on foot. After Saul's conversion, he began to preach in the synagogues of Damascus. He reported that he escaped arrest in Damascus because he "was let down in a basket through a window in the wall" (2 Corinthians 11:33).

Acts 13:9 says that Saul was also known as Paul, and from that point on, the name *Paul* is used to refer to him. Only when Paul tells the story of the con-version experience does Acts record Paul referring to himself as Saul, thus many associate the name *Paul* with Saul's new life. The Book of Acts does not, however, explicitly name this as the reason for the shift to the name *Paul*.

Acts is the second volume of a two-vol-ume work. Luke is the first volume, and Acts continues the story of what hap-pened after Christ's ascension. As follow-ers of Jesus spread out across the landscape, the movement grew, taking root among different cultures and various peoples.

A LIGHT FROM HEAVEN

A LIGHT FROM HEAVEN

✳ Talk about what you think happened to Saul on the road to Damascus. How would you explain the experience? What do you think he saw and heard? What do you think he felt or thought at the time?

Illustrate the conversion. Read the text again slowly. Have colored markers and paper ready. While the text is being read, create a picture of what Saul experienced as you see it in your imagination. Tell about your illustration.

Write in your journal about what you think Saul experienced and about transforming moments in your own life.

Saul, "still breathing threats and murder" against followers of Jesus, started off for Damascus, a journey that would change his life and the shape of what would become the Christian faith. This story may be a famous conversion story, but it is dispassionately told. The storyteller does not embellish, but writes in a straightforward way about the events. Over-dramatization is not necessary. On the road to Damascus something of God occurred. A great light from heaven flashed around Saul, and he could do nothing but fall to the ground at the intensity of the light. People in the Bible often encountered God in association with some form of light.

The accounts of Saul's conversion vary in their descriptions of what the traveling companions saw or heard. In Acts 9:7, they saw nothing but they heard the voices; in Acts 22:9, they saw the light but heard nothing; and in Acts 26:13-14, the light fell over all of them and Saul heard the voice. The voice calls out, "Saul, Saul, why do you persecute me?" Saul wanted to know who this was speaking to him. He addressed him as Lord, which in this sense is a term of respect like *sir*. The voice identified itself as

74

Jesus. Because Saul was persecuting followers of Jesus, he was, in fact, persecuting Jesus. Jesus instructed Saul to get up and to go into the city where he would be told what to do. Saul got up, and though his eyes were opened, he could not see. The others led him to Damascus. His blindness continued for three days, and he neither ate nor drank.

ON THE ROAD AGAIN

The story of the road to Damascus is one of several "road stories" in the Bible. Another is the story of the walk to Emmaus when the risen Jesus appeared to two of his followers. Often, in the Bible and in contemporary life, an experience of the divine occurs while going somewhere or while in transition from one way of life into another. Many of us do not like to be in a state of transition. We do not like to move or be in-between jobs or unsettled in any way. Yet, these transitional times provide prime opportunities for God to break in. People often come to God while going through a divorce, coming to the end of a career, losing a loved one, or waiting for the results of a medical test. Being on our way somewhere provides an occasion to "see the light." New things are revealed to us. The metaphor of pilgrimage, of moving toward God, is rich in meaning. An old Japanese proverb declares, "The journey is also the destination." William Sloan Coffin wrote:

ON THE ROAD AGAIN

❁ Think about times you have experienced God while in transition. When have you grown close to God while moving, traveling, or waiting for something? Write about these experiences in your journal, then talk about them with the whole group.

❁ Create a mural. Identify other road stories in the Bible (examples: Abraham and Sarah, the Hebrews in the wilderness, Jacob's return home after fleeing his brother's wrath). Review what happens in these stories and what transformations occur. Take a long sheet of paper and draw a winding road from one end to the other. Put the heading "On the Road in the Bible" at the top. Illustrate several Bible stories that tell of God's revelation to a person or persons while they are moving from place to place. Label each illustration to identify the Bible story.

Read the William Sloan Coffin quotation aloud. Do you agree with his assessment of the Christian life? Why or why not?

We are a pilgrim people, a people who have decided never to arrive, a people who live by hope, energized not by what we already possess, but by that which is promised.[1]

So it was with Saul. While on his way to persecute more Christians, Saul saw the light and heard the voice of Jesus. The end of the road in Damascus really was not the end; it was a new beginning.

Whether it is sudden, as it was with Saul, or gradual, a conversion experience is a call to a new life. For Saul it was the beginning of his missionary journeys to spread Christianity throughout the world. Conversion is not the end of the story for any Christian. It is not simply an individual, personal attainment.

Conversion leads a person into membership in the Christian community. Henri Nouwen (in *With Open Hands*, Ave Maria Press, page 114) wrote: "Conversion to God, therefore, means a simultaneous conversion to the other persons who live with you on this earth."

ANANIAS

✱ Discuss how God used Ananias to bring about Saul's healing. Would you have been able to do what Ananias did? Who in your own life reminds you of Ananias? What are the scales that need to fall from our own eyes?

ANANIAS

The story continues in Damascus when the Lord appeared to Ananias in a vision. The Lord told Ananias to go to Straight Street to the house of Judas to find Saul who was at that very moment seeing a vision of Ananias laying hands on him.

Ananias resisted, citing Saul's reputation as a persecutor. The Lord, however, told him again to go, for he was a "chosen instrument" (*vessel* in some translations). Ironically, the one who caused suffering for those who called upon the name of Jesus would now suffer for that name. Saul's mission was to carry the name of Jesus before Gentiles, kings, and the people of Israel (9:15). Obediently, Ananias went and laid hands on the weakened Saul, calling him "brother"; and Saul received the Holy Spirit. Then we are told that something like scales fell from Saul's eyes and he could see again. The scales are those things that blind us, whatever they may be. When they fall off, we can see again in a new way. Saul had been blind to the truth of Christ, but he was healed, both physically and inwardly. Saul got up, was baptized, and took something to eat.

THE NEW SAUL

THE NEW SAUL

❀ Talk about conversion. What are some different kinds of conversion experiences? When have you been blasted out of your belief system because of something beyond your control? In what ways can conversion be gradual?

Over the next several days Saul went from persecuting the early followers of Jesus to proclaiming Jesus as the Son of God. His experience overwhelmed him and he was blasted out of his belief system by something outside of his control. His zeal and personality were not changed; they were re-directed.

A conversion experience may be described as undergoing a transformation when confronted with truth. It is not simply a moral reformation, not simply a

77

❀ Add descriptive words to the "After" silhouette of Saul. Display the "Before" and "After" silhouettes side by side.

Read a spiritual autobiography over the next several weeks. Choose a person who has written the story of his or her spiritual journey such as Teresa of Avila; C. S. Lewis; Martin Luther King, Jr.; Jane Goodall; Maya Angelou; Corrie Ten Boom; Anne Lamott; Billy Graham; or others. Plan a follow-up session to report on these and discuss them. How are their stories like or unlike your own?

change from being bad to being good. Being a Christian is not just about being a "good person." Becoming a Christian results from reorienting one's life to God who is made known through Jesus Christ. One of the results of that experience of reorientation may be a change in behavior. In response to this profound experience, Saul did change his ways. Those who knew him before found it difficult to believe that he was the same person (9:21). God can bring such radical transformation that God can and does use flawed individuals, even murderers, persecutors, and prostitutes.

Such conversion experiences often compel a person to talk to others about the experience. Paul describes his experience again in Acts 22:1-15 and 26:1-23. When people are transformed by God's light, they often feel a need to tell others about the change that has overcome previous perceptions and has inspired new ways of living.

Music and artistic expression are other ways that people share their newfound faith. A number of losses in his life, including the death of his wife, led Rembrandt to turn away from licentious behavior to paint *The Return of the Prodigal Son*. Bluegrass great, Bill Monroe sings the song, "I Saw the Light." Hymns that witness to conversion or to a transforming experience are, "O Happy Day, That Fixed My Choice," "Freely, Freely," "Ask Ye What Great

Thing I Know," and "Come, O Thou Traveler Unknown."

STRANGELY WARMED

We have heard about other conversion experiences, some dramatic, and some extraordinary in their simplicity. Theologian Bernard Lonergan compared the experience of religious conversion to falling in love. Saint Augustine converted to Christianity following many years as an egotistical rhetorician who pursued various pagan philosophies. C. S. Lewis left the Christian faith of his youth and became an atheist before his conversion back to Christianity. Mary Clarke was a wealthy Beverly Hills socialite who, after her marriage of twenty-five years ended, became a nun and felt a call from God to minister to prisoners in Mexico. She became Sister Antonia and founded an order called Servants of the Eleventh Hour for women who come to their Christian vocation late in life after being widowed or divorced.

John Wesley was impressed with the faith of the Moravians when he traveled with them by ship to minister in Georgia. When he returned, disappointed with his efforts and discouraged in his own spiritual life, he attended a prayer meeting. He described the experience:

> I felt my heart strangely warmed. I felt I did trust in Christ, Christ alone for salvation; and an assurance was given

STRANGELY WARMED

❋ Hold a love feast or *agape* (ah-GAH-pay) meal. Bring in cookies or sweet rolls and water. Create your own service by writing prayers, singing hymns, and giving testimonies. Take a collection for the poor. Talk about mountaintop or "strangely warmed" experiences you have had.

me that He had taken away my sins, even mine, and saved me from the law of sin and death (Wesley's Journal entry; May 24, 1738).

Actually, this was one of several transformative experiences of Wesley's life. These experiences did not mean that he no longer had doubts but that when he was at important crossroads in his life, he became aware of God's converting grace.

Feelings of religious joy and elation, sometimes referred to as "mountaintop experiences," often lead to further spiritual growth when nurtured properly in the faith.

AMAZING GRACE

Different people come to know Christ in different ways. Some grow up as Christians, in devout families that regularly attend church and practice holiness at home. Others grow up in unchurched families and come to know Christ through conversation with other Christians. Some become aware of their salvation as a gradual process. Others undergo a dramatic conversion experience, going from the pits to the mountaintop. Some experience a sense of peace after going through inner turmoil.

Many of us experience several transformations in our journey. I once heard conversion compared to handling a horse. Some break a horse all at once, getting up at dawn and working with the horse all day or as long as it takes until it will take

AMAZING GRACE
Plan a retreat. Decide on a future date and place for a day-long retreat. Arrange for someone to lead the retreat. Use retreat models from *A Guide to Retreat for All God's Shepherds*, by Rueben P. Job (Abingdon Press, 1994).

❄ Tell the story of John Newton. Sing "Amazing Grace," or listen to a recording of the song. Mahalia Jackson's CD entitled *Amazing Grace* is a good choice. Cite examples of God's amazing grace.

Arrange ahead of time for two or three people to come in and share how they came to know Christ. Try to get people whose experiences vary. Discuss how a mountaintop experience changes us in the eyes of our friends and family. Tell about other conversion experiences of well-known Christians you have read about.

a saddle and bridle. Others work with the horse slowly, over a long period of time, to accustom the animal to the bridle and bit.

Many may be familiar with the story of hymn writer John Newton. John Newton went to sea with his father when he was eleven years old. He endured many hardships and difficult times. As a young man he joined the crew of a slave ship and later became the captain of his own slave ship, capturing and selling human beings for money. John Newton, while still a slave-trader had occasion to hear the preaching of George Whitefield and the Wesleys. At the age of thirty he converted and pursued holy orders. He was an ordained Anglican priest when he penned the well-loved hymn, *Amazing Grace*:

Amazing grace! How sweet the sound
that saved a wretch like me!
I once was lost, but now am found;
was blind, but now I see.

John Newton testified that even though he had once been an infidel and a sinner, God changed him.[2] The hymn speaks to our personal sense of wretchedness that can be relieved only by the experience of God's grace and saving power in our lives. It assures us that God can and does work change in the hearts of humankind.

APOSTLE OF LIGHT
❄ Look up Romans 1:1, 5 and think about what was ahead for

APOSTLE OF LIGHT

Paul, known earlier as Saul, came to be "a servant of Jesus Christ" and an apostle,

Paul. How did he go from persecutor of Christians to carry the gospel message throughout the Mediterranean world? How was he an apostle of light?

Read aloud 2 Corinthians 4:4-6. Who is the god of this world? How can we do as Paul suggests? How can we reflect God's light?

❀ Be an apostle of light. Plan to continue to bring God's light to others. Give each person a bright yellow flame cut from construction paper. Write one thing each will do to bring forth God's light as a result of this study. Tell participants to take the flame home and tape it to the refrigerator, or put it in a place you will see it.

"set apart for the gospel of God" (see Romans 1:1, 5). He engaged in collecting contributions from Gentiles to support the church in Jerusalem, as evidence of his sincerity. When the collection was complete, he delivered it and began to plan to go elsewhere to carry the gospel message. It was his mission to carry the light to the world. He was sent to be a "light to the Gentiles" (Acts 13:47). Paul's journey was an incredible one consisting of imprisonment, shipwreck, and conflict. We are privy to some of his letters that are included in the New Testament.

Paul urged people to "lay aside the works of darkness" and to "put on the armor of light" (Romans 13:12). Paul is a model to us of how we can reflect the light of Jesus Christ to others. He summed up his message using the familiar imagery of light in the Second Letter to the Corinthians:

> In their case the god of this world has blinded the minds of the unbelievers, to keep them from seeing the light of the gospel of the glory of Christ, who is the image of God. For we do not proclaim ourselves; we proclaim Jesus Christ as Lord and ourselves as your slaves for Jesus' sake. For it is the God who said, "Let light shine out of darkness," who has shone in our hearts to give the light of the knowledge of the glory of God in the face of Jesus Christ.
> —2 Corinthians 4:4-6

CLOSING TIME

❀ Take a word association test. Call out the following words. Ask persons to write the word or phrase that first comes to mind: *light; darkness; reflect; fire; water; God; conversion; apostle of light.*

❀ Review the characters in the sessions: Moses, Nehemiah, Mary, the shepherds, Simeon, Nicodemus, Saul. How did they serve God? How were they transformed by God's light? What did you learn in this study?

Write a prayer of thanksgiving including the actions of the biblical characters. Pray this in your closing worship. As:

God, light in our darkness, we remember Nicodemus who in his own resistance taught us to give ourselves openly to Jesus.

❀ Form a quartet or sing in unison "I Saw the Light" (wearing sunglasses of course!). Remove the sunglasses and sing "Amazing Grace."

CLOSING TIME

As we come to the end of the study, I invite you to reflect upon what God has revealed to you through the Scriptures. I invite you to go into the world with the light of God's countenance upon you and with a renewed determination to let that light shine for others. Rejoice with Simeon as he praised God in the Temple:

Lord, now let your servants go in peace; your word has been fulfilled: our own eyes have seen the salvation that you have prepared in the presence of all people, a light to reveal you to the nations and the glory of your people Israel.

—adapted from Luke 2:29-32

---

[1] William Sloan Coffin quoted in *Inspiration: 2000 Years of Christian Wisdom*. Nashville: Dimensions for Living, 2001, page 60.

[2] Dennis E. Smith and Michael E. Williams, eds., *Storyteller's Companion to the Bible: The Acts of the Apostles*. Vol. 12, Nashville: Abingdon Press, 1999, pages 76–77.

INTERGENERATIONAL ACTIVITIES

Plan a church-wide worship service. Have all ages involved as liturgists and singers. Explain the display you have added to each session, talking about what each item represents. Display art projects from each session.

Create a puppet show depicting Saul's conversion on the road to Damascus. Write a script, make stick puppets, and perform the show.

Have a light fest. On a clear night string Christmas lights in your parking lot or church yard. Invite your neighbors for games and fellowship. Play flashlight tag. Serve lemonade or home-made ice cream.

Hold a candlelight prayer vigil. Decide on what you will pray for. Some suggestions include peace in the Middle East or an end to child abuse. Gather participants in a public place and pass out candles. Lead in prayer and singing.